THE ENGLISH UTILITARIANS

THE ENGLISH UTILITARIANS

By JOHN PLAMENATZ

BASIL BLACKWELL
OXFORD
1958

© Basil Blackwell & Mott, Ltd., 1958

First printed 1949
Second, revised edition 1958

Printed in Great Britain for BASIL BLACKWELL & MOTT, LTD.
by A. R. MOWBRAY & Co. LIMITED in the City of Oxford
and bound at the KEMP HALL BINDERY

EDITOR'S NOTE TO THE SECOND EDITION

AN entirely new chapter, the longest of all, has been added to the second edition of this book. The author thought it best to leave the chapters of the first edition as they were, except for minor alterations. In the additional chapter he has corrected mistakes made in the first edition, and has also used several new arguments, both against Bentham and his school and in their favour. He has tried to show that the inadequacy of theories like Bentham's lies above all in their quite false conception of what is involved in being a social and moral creature, and can still remain even when hedonism and egoism are abandoned. With this purpose in mind, he has compared utilitarian and idealist conceptions, not to prove the second superior to the first, but to reveal the strong and the weak points of both. He has also argued that, starting from utilitarian premises alone, it is not possible to make a convincing case for democracy; and in the course of the argument has examined Bentham's assertion that every man is apt to be the best judge of his own interest.

The additional chapter goes, he hopes, more deeply into the utilitarian philosophy than any of the chapters of the first edition.

J.P.

March, 1958

CONTENTS

THE
ENGLISH UTILITARIANS

CHAPTER I

THE THEORY AND ITS ORIGINS

1. THE THEORY DEFINED

THERE is scarcely a writer on moral and political theory who is free from every taint of utilitarianism. Since all men often seek pleasure and avoid pain, no one anxious to have an audience will preach complete indifference to either. That is why the more enthusiastic utilitarians have sometimes been tempted to assert that all men are with them even when they think otherwise. Bentham never doubted that when the nonsense is eliminated from rival theories, what remains behind is always his own. James Mill was inclined to believe that when others thought they disagreed with him they were, without knowing it, caught up in the intricacies of language. He believed that all men are utilitarians in practice, though many of them, having illusions of which they cannot get rid, are unwilling to admit it. Whether the utilitarian theory is true or false, it is at least plausible. In one form or another, it occurs readily enough to anyone who reflects on the moral or political behaviour of mankind. There can be little purpose, then, in noticing the many traces of the doctrine to be found in a great variety of European philosophies. What is profitable is not to discover the sense in which all men are utilitarians, but to define the doctrine so narrowly that only those thinkers who are usually called utilitarians deserve the name.

The utilitarians, properly so called, flourished in this country for a period of over a hundred years, from the middle of the eighteenth to the middle of the nineteenth century. There were also utilitarians in France and in other parts of Europe, but the doctrine is essentially

English. Indeed, in its many varieties, it constitutes the largest
contribution made by the English to moral and political theory.
It is intimately connected with English empiricism, although there
is no logical necessity in the connexion. And if the greatest of
English political philosophers was not a utilitarian, he exercised the
most powerful influence on those who were. Bentham and James
Mill lived in the shadow of Hobbes all their intellectual lives and
Hume learnt more from him than he ever acknowledged.
M. Halévy, in his book on *Philosophic Radicalism*, found much to
say about continental utilitarians. But in spite of M. Halévy, it is,
I think, possible to confine one's attention to English writers and to
miss very little that is important. And that little is to be found in
Helvetius and Beccaria.

The four most important utilitarians are Hume, Bentham, James
Mill and his son, John Stuart Mill. What is it that is common to
all their theories? Part of the answer to this question is the definition
of utilitarianism. But I hope, in this essay, to do more than just
define the doctrine; I hope also to give the reader an idea of the
great variety and richness of the systems of which it forms a part.

I had better begin with a short definition of the utilitarian
doctrine. It seems to me that all its adherents assert or assume
(more often the latter) the truth of the following propositions:

(i) Pleasure is alone good or desirable for its own sake; or else
men call only those things good that are pleasant or a means to
what is pleasant.

(ii) The equal pleasures of any two or more men are equally
good.

(iii) No action is right unless it appears to the agent to be the
action most likely, under the circumstances, to produce the greatest
happiness; or else men do not call any action right unless it is one of
a type that usually produces the greatest happiness possible under
the circumstances.

(iv) Men's obligations to the government of the country in which
they live, and that government's duties to them, have nothing to
do with the way in which the government first acquired power or
now maintains it, except to the extent to which these origins and
methods affect its ability to carry out these duties.

I must first insist that this definition is not a precise statement of
the opinions common to all the utilitarians. To offer precision

where there is no place for it is only to mislead. Every one of the four propositions set out above can be interpreted in several different ways. Indeed, had this not been so, they would have been useless for my purpose.

In case I should be accused of paradox, I must explain my meaning. In the sphere of morals and politics, a definition, to be precise, would have to be indefinitely long; and to be useful as well as precise, it would have to be, not one definition, but many, of which each gave one of the meanings of the term in question. Now, my business is not to define terms precisely but to set a limit to their possible definitions. Though the utilitarians aimed at clarity and consistency, and came nearer to achieving both than most philosophers have done, they used, when they discussed morals and politics, the old vocabulary that had served so many purposes in its time. No one can know what exactly they meant when they used this vocabulary. The reader is therefore to understand no more than this: that, in my opinion, anyone may properly be called a utilitarian if he believes that these four propositions are true, provided only that his interpretation of them does no violence to the usual meanings of the words they contain. There are many questions that most of the utilitarians never bothered to ask. What are pleasure and pain? Are they capable of measurement? If they are not, is there still some sense in which one pleasure or pain may be said to be greater, equal to or less than another? What is implied by the statement that pleasure is good and pain evil? A man may, if he has the necessary training in logic, make a long list of the senses in which the utilitarians may have used any one of their favourite words or phrases. But whatever the answers to these questions, and the lists prepared by our imaginary logician, there are limits to what the utilitarians could have meant. And these limits are set, not merely or even primarily by the definitions they themselves offer, but by the uses to which they put some of the commonest words in the vocabulary of the moralist and the politician.

I hope my definition is adequate, but I know it cannot be and believe it ought not to be precise. Even if, since their time, ethics and politics had acquired a precise vocabulary, it would be difficult to use it to describe the doctrines of the utilitarians; for their doctrines would not lend themselves to such treatment. To use a scientific vocabulary to define unscientific notions is like trying to chop wood with a razor; there is no end to the work, and the instrument, improperly used, is soon blunted. But there, in fact, exists no scientific vocabulary for the use of the political and moral philosopher. He must make do with words that are among the most frequently used in every language. When he is trying to describe the phenomena that constitute the moral and political behaviour of mankind, his disadvantage, if he understands its nature, is almost intolerable. But when his task is to describe doctrines, put together in their time by men no better provided than himself, he need not feel unequal to it. The same rough methods that suited them must also be good enough for him. And there is this much to be said for the utilitarians, that, though they did not speak like scientists, they always spoke sensibly. They were content with as much elasticity in the language as it naturally possessed. They did not distort or inflate it. They used it like Englishmen and not like philosophers, and so they never did to it the almost irreparable damage which, if we are to believe some Germans, was done to their language by philosophers. Even Bentham had a proper instinct in this matter; he wanted to create a technical vocabulary separate from the one in ordinary use.

Though these four propositions give us, as I believe, the essence of utilitarianism, this does not mean that the utilitarians do not often make statements inconsistent with them; that is to say, inconsistent with any reasonable interpretation of them. They do so either because they are not aware of the inconsistencies involved or else because they think they are making qualifications of only minor importance. These four propositions, in the sum of their usual meanings, embrace most of the beliefs to which the utilitarians attach the greatest importance and which they most often assert or assume. This is, I think, as much as can be expected of a set of propositions, not too complicated to be useful, and intended to cover the essential doctrines of a numerous school of philosophers. A definition of this kind is like the great bed at Ware, that will hold all the members of a large family, though the limbs of one or two of them hang over its sides.

There are two further points about this definition that call for comment. In the first place, so far as this definition goes, a utilitarian theory of morals may or may not be what Professor G. E.

Moore has called naturalistic. By a 'naturalistic' theory of morals Professor Moore means any theory that asserts or assumes that goodness denotes some property, simple or complex, of a natural object. And by a natural object he means anything that is the subject matter of the natural sciences.[1] I do not think that Professor Moore has made his meaning clear. Goodness, whatever it is and even if his account of it is correct, must be a property of what exists, and nothing does exist, if we are to believe Professor Moore, except natural objects. What Professor Moore probably means is that a theory of morals is naturalistic if it asserts or assumes that goodness is a property of which any natural science takes account. Or in other words, a theory of morals is naturalistic if it reduces ethics to a branch of psychology, sociology or any of the other natural sciences. Professor Moore himself believes that ethics is not a natural science, and that goodness is a simple, indefinable, unanalysable quality that is neither a constituent nor a relational, but a resultant, property of the things called good. A resultant property is, he thinks, neither spatial nor temporal, though what it belongs to may be the latter or both. Professor Moore believes that anyone who disagrees with him, who asserts, for instance, that good means pleasant or approved of or desired (however many qualifications are introduced for the sake of plausibility), is guilty of what he calls the naturalistic fallacy. He is guilty of assuming that goodness is the same thing as some one or other of the properties always or often possessed by the things called good, these properties being constituent or relational. Professor Moore himself thinks that goodness, alone of moral notions, is simple and indefinable, rightness being no more than conduciveness to what is good. But it is possible to be as absolute about the one notion as the other, and to insist, as some moralists have done, that they are both simple and indefinable.

Now, I will not say that the utilitarians are guilty of the naturalistic fallacy, for, unless Professor Moore is right, there can be no such fallacy. But it is very probable that most of their theories are, in his sense of that word, naturalistic. They would, most of them, had they considered the matter, probably have denied that there are such simple unanalysable qualities, different in kind from all others, as Professor Moore would have *goodness* to be, and other

[1] *Principia Ethica*, pp. 40–1 (1903 edition).

philosophers *rightness* as well. But though it is very probable that they would, most of them, have denied this, it would still have been a mistake to define their doctrine in such a way as to entail this denial. Professor Moore's distinction was never present to the minds of the utilitarians. It would therefore be misleading to define the doctrine in such a way as would suggest that they all made the same answer to a question never put by any of them. Of the major utilitarians, Hume and James Mill alone express themselves so clearly and consistently that it is never possible, for one moment, to doubt that their theories are naturalistic. But Bentham, with his usual lack of interest in a distinction from which no important practical consequences are to be drawn, speaks with many voices. There are times when he talks as if good and pleasant meant the same thing; at other times his words suggest that good means desired or approved of; and at still other times, what he says would be nonsense unless he were understood to mean that good and desirable are synonymous. Bentham is more concerned with the notion of rightness than goodness, and his usual account of it is that it is the same thing as utility. But he also often implies that it is not, that rightness and utility, though inseparably connected, are different. For he calls utility the criterion of morality, which is to suggest that they are two and not one. Yet the most cautious man, though he might say that doubts about Bentham are permissible, would hazard the guess that, on this question, he shares the opinion of Hume and James Mill. The most difficult case is that of John Stuart Mill. His general philosophy requires that his moral theory should be naturalistic, and the principles on which he rests that theory are in fact naturalistic, but some of the modifications he introduces at later stages in his argument are hardly to be reconciled with these principles. This does not mean that they cannot be reconciled with other principles which, though they are not utilitarian, are naturalistic; and in fact I believe that they can. There is, indeed, better reason for believing that the younger Mill's theory is consistently naturalistic than that it is consistently utilitarian. And in any case his fundamental principles are clearly both. For he tells us that rightness is conduciveness to pleasure, and also that to think of a thing as desirable is to think of it as pleasant. But though it is highly probable that the moral theories of the four greatest utilitarians are naturalistic, it is impossible to hold that none of the others differs from them in this respect. Godwin, for instance, asserts that justice is eternal, and by this assertion he seems to mean that it follows from the very fact that sentient and intelligent beings are living together that it is the duty of each, whatever his desires and emotions, to promote to the best of his ability the happiness of the others. This being so, it follows that the greatest happiness of the greatest number is an end desirable for its own sake, and that morals can never be reduced to a branch of psychology or of any other of the natural sciences. That sentient and intelligent beings ought to act in this way is, apparently, a proposition whose truth is borne in upon us as soon as we have understood it. The notion of obligation expressed in this proposition is not to be explained in terms of human desires or feelings. It is simple and unanalysable, just as Professor Moore supposes goodness to be. Godwin does not tell us this, but it is what his theory implies. For though he, like every other utilitarian, knows nothing of a distinction first made by Professor Moore, and is not even aware that the ultimate principle from which he starts is different from any advocated by Hume, whose general philosophy he accepts, it is clear that his moral theory is not naturalistic. And what is clearly true of Godwin may also be true of several other utilitarians, who are even less anxious than he to discuss the logical status of their fundamental principles. No more need, I think, be said to show that it would be a mistake so to define utilitarianism as to suggest that every utilitarian theory must be naturalistic.

More important, when we discuss the utilitarians, is the distinction between those who say that the criterion of morality is objective and those who believe that actions are right or wrong only because they are approved or disapproved by all or most of the persons who contemplate them. Hume belongs clearly to the latter class; Bentham, and those in the intellectual descent from him, to the former. But even this distinction does not enable us to place every utilitarian in one of two classes, for it is a distinction without interest to many of them.

In the second place, this definition of the utilitarian doctrine excludes the theory of morals called egoistic hedonism, whose most famous English exponent is Hobbes. It cannot be said that Hobbes, in the same sense as Hume, Bentham and the Mills, regards one man's pleasure as equally valuable with any other's. Hobbes says no more than that a man desires only his own pleasure, and that whatever he desires he calls good. Since every man desires his own pleasure, it follows that every human pleasure is called good by some man. Hobbes might therefore say that any man's pleasure is just as good as any other man's. But this is not the sense in which, according to the utilitarians, one man's pleasure is as good as another's. For the utilitarian regards the greatest happiness of the greatest number as in itself desirable. If this means anything, it implies that it is as much a man's duty to give pleasure to other people as to secure it for himself. But Hobbes's system implies no such thing. The greatest happiness of the greatest number as the supreme end of human action can mean nothing to Hobbes. A man will seek other men's pleasures only as a means to his own, and he will call no pleasures good except his own. If, in the order of possible worlds, his own happiness varied inversely with that of other men, he would call that world best in which the sum of human misery was the greatest.

It is true that several utilitarians, including Bentham and James Mill, adopt, either occasionally or invariably, the egoistic hedonism of Hobbes. And many others, though they say nothing definite, use language that suggests that it is somehow more obviously right that a man should seek his own pleasure than other people's. Egoism, they appear to assume, stands in no need of either explanation or justification, but altruism does. And in their attempt to justify it, they suggest that altruism arises out of egoism, or else that it is a subtle and refined form of it. But for all this, they do not cease to be utilitarians. They either make an attempt to reconcile their egoistic hedonism with their belief that the end of all human action ought to be the greatest possible happiness, no matter whose, or else they believe that the two doctrines are so obviously compatible that no reconciliation is necessary. In any case, what they are primarily interested in advocating and defending is some form or other of utilitarianism. It can be said of them all, even of James Mill, that at heart they are utilitarians, though their minds are full of the prejudices to which Hobbes gave such striking expression. Only Hume and the utilitarians who, like Adam Smith, follow closely in his footsteps, succeed in avoiding the traps laid for future generations in the *Leviathan*. And even Hume, who finds it easy to accord to altruism a separate existence in its own right, continually insists on the predominant selfishness of man.

Utilitarianism and egoism are, of course, incompatible doctrines. If men desire only their own pleasure, or if their own pleasure is all they ought to desire, there can be no sense in saying that the greatest happiness of the greatest number is desirable. Even if it were true that no man could attain his own greatest happiness unless all other men did the same, it would still be impossible to reconcile egoism and utilitarianism. For it must still follow, if egoism is true, that nothing can be desired or desirable, except each man's happiness by himself, so that the greatest happiness of the greatest number neither can nor ought to be desired by any man for all men's sake but only for his own. No harmony of interests, natural or contrived, can effect a reconciliation between the two doctrines, though, should such a harmony exist, it cannot be important which of the two doctrines is true. For in that case, what the enlightened egoist desires as a means is desired as an end by the enlightened utilitarian; and whichever of the two realizes his desire, mankind are equally happy. But though it may well be that, under certain ideal circumstances, it is practically indifferent which of the two doctrines is true, this does not alter the fact that they cannot, under any conceivable circumstances, both be true.

Now, it cannot be denied that Bentham and James Mill asserted that both are true, and James Mill at least attempted to reconcile each with the other. The attempt was, of course, unsuccessful, but this lack of success is no reason for denying that the elder Mill was a utilitarian. Had he not believed that utilitarianism is true, he could not have wished to reconcile egoistic hedonism with it. Nor, I think, should we deny the name utilitarian to Bentham, who never felt the need to effect such a reconciliation. It never even occurred to him that the two doctrines might appear incompatible, since he was the happy possessor of both. It was his mission in life to teach men how they might contrive a harmony of selfish interests, so that it might at last be possible for them to desire as a means what they ought to promote for its own sake. The suspicion that an end so defined is a contradiction in terms never entered the head of this practical man. He may not have known how to define it but he knew what he wanted; and had he achieved it, it would not have mattered how he defined it. Bentham and James

B

Mill were egoistic hedonists. But this is a fact about them much
less important than that they were also utilitarians. It is the utilitarian doctrine that is the major premise of all their favourite
practical arguments. And that it is so is not a matter of indifference,
for until a harmony of selfish interests is established, egoism and
utilitarianism cannot justify the same rules of conduct. But it was
the rules justified by utilitarianism that they both wished to
establish. Hobbes tried to prove that one of the necessary means to
each man's happiness, the existence of a sovereign able to enforce
obedience to his commands, is also the means to other men's
happiness. Neither Bentham nor Mill would have denied this.
But Hobbes never justified the institution of the sovereign on the
ground that the harmony of interests created by it must increase
the sum of human happiness. Bentham and Mill, on the other hand,
wished to establish a more perfect harmony than any conceived by
Hobbes for precisely this reason. They did not say: let everyone
strive to create a harmony of selfish interests, for until it is created he
cannot hope to be happy. They said: the best society is the one in
which there is the greatest happiness of the greatest number, and
we must therefore strive to create a harmony of selfish interests, for
unless we do so, this desirable end cannot be achieved. This is the
great difference between Hobbes and the two utilitarians who came
closest to an uncritical acceptance of his doctrines; and in virtue of
it, it is but just that they should be called utilitarians and he always
an egoist.

2. Hobbes and the Utilitarians

Hobbes had a bad reputation and later philosophers were not
anxious to acknowledge their debt to him. But in the *Leviathan*
there is such an abundance of riches that several generations could
borrow freely from it and be satisfied. It is not difficult, in spite of
their discreet silence, to see how much the utilitarians owe to
Hobbes.

Hobbes did not invent all the theories that are to-day so strongly
associated with his name. No man can be an innovator on such a
scale. But Hobbes did step aside from the European tradition of his
day. He put his questions differently and gave different answers.
The extent of the difference is disguised by his political vocabulary,
which is less unlike that of other men than his ideas.

From the time of Plato until that of Hobbes, two sorts of moral theory had prevailed among European philosophers. The one makes the supreme object of human endeavour the full and harmonious development of all the powers of the individual; while the other declares that virtue consists in behaviour according to rules that man can discover by the use of his reason. These two kinds of theories can be combined in many ways and they can also be related to many different conceptions of the universe. It can, for instance, be said that a man will 'realize' himself, will become the best that he has it in him to be, if he behaves according to the laws of nature revealed to him by his reason. Or it can be said, as it was by Plato and Aristotle, that man will attain his full development only in the perfectly constituted state. Nor is there anything to prevent a man from saying that the laws of reason are the laws of God. Some philosophers have been loath to reject any part of what they considered to be the inherited and divinely inspired wisdom of mankind. Such a philosopher was St. Thomas Aquinas, in whose house there are many mansions in which all the great thinkers of the past are honourably received.

Respect for the past and hospitality to its traditions are not among the virtues of Hobbes. He finds no room for any essential part of either of the two most important European moral philosophies. According to his system, no man can be better or worse than he was before; he can only be more or less successful in acquiring felicity. Nor are there any rules which all men, who have the use of their reason, discover to be binding upon themselves merely because they are rational and sentient beings and live in society with others like themselves. The laws of morality, in the opinion of Hobbes, have no such validity; they are merely rules that men, since they wish to be happy, would do well to obey, provided that other men do likewise. The state is no more than a contrivance to ensure that all men do obey these rules, so that it may be the interest of each of them to do so. For a man who obeys them, while others do not, is no better than a fool.

The utilitarians share with Hobbes a complete indifference to the notion of self-improvement as a thing desirable for its own sake. The single exception is John Stuart Mill, but this is merely one of several ways in which he is untrue to the doctrine inherited from his father. The later utilitarians are as great enthusiasts as Plato for education, but its only purpose, in their opinion, is to make men more efficient producers of happiness. And like Hobbes, all the utilitarians, with the exception, once again, of John Stuart Mill, that unhappy and unconscious traitor to their creed, deny that virtue, which is obedience to the moral law, has a value for men independent of its power to promote their happiness.

The influence of Hobbes on some utilitarians is much greater than on others. The man of virtue, for both Hobbes and Bentham, is the excellent calculator. Nor are the calculations they advocate very different from one another. Though Bentham's supreme end can mean nothing to Hobbes, yet the actions that promote it are those most likely to make the agents themselves happy. Bentham's legislator makes the laws that ensure that each man from selfish motives will promote the greatest happiness of the greatest number; while Hobbes's sovereign ensures that each man will pursue his own happiness unmolested by the others. The two philosophers define their terms differently, but the sort of considerations that they think ought to weigh with men when they act are pretty much alike.

It is in the sphere of political philosophy that Hobbes has the most direct and obvious influence on the utilitarians, even on Hume, whose theory of morals, except in its rejection of the two great European traditions, is so unlike that of the *Leviathan*. The utilitarians, like Hobbes, regard the state as a means of reconciling men's selfish interests. It exists, not to protect their rights, but to give men more abundantly the happiness they always seek. Hobbes, it is true, speaks of 'natural rights' that men possess before they enter political society, but he does not mean by this phrase what others have meant who used it. When Hobbes says that, in the state of nature, men have an unlimited right to acquire whatever takes their fancy provided they have the strength to do so, he can only mean that, outside society, there is no sense in saying that it would be wrong for them to take it. Right for Hobbes is therefore mere absence of wrong. But when we say that a man has a right to do something, we imply that it would be wrong for other men to try to prevent him. This is also implied by what most philosophers, who use the term, say of natural rights. But the case with Hobbes is different. He uses the phrase in a meaning all his own. The natural rights of Hobbes are not rights at all, and no state can exist for their protection.

Hobbes misleads his reader, and perhaps also himself, by his account of the sovereign's institution, of which he says that it involves the transfer of their natural rights by the persons who form a political society to the man who is to be their sovereign. Now, a natural right of the sort described by Hobbes cannot be transferred. Though the men who agree to form a political society so act that one man among them can exercise effectively over the others the power that they, all of them, in the state of nature vainly tried to exercise, there is no transference of power, let alone of right. For the power that belongs to the sovereign in political society belonged to no one in the state of nature. What Hobbes has done is to call powers rights and then treat them as if they were what other people call by that name. Natural rights, in the traditional sense, are as unnecessary to Hobbes's political philosophy as to that of any of the utilitarians.

Though Hobbes describes the transfer of rights and speaks of the sovereign as bearing the 'persons' of his subjects, the whole of his long account of the matter is foreign to the main body of his doctrines. It is a piece of mysticism that can mean nothing to whoever has accepted the other parts of his theory. There is no sense compatible with Hobbes's premises in which the sovereign can do no wrong and his subjects can do it. If a subject finds it his interest to obey the laws, while the sovereign can often afford, when it suits his purpose, to ignore them, this is only because the subject has little power and the sovereign a great deal. Hobbes's principles once accepted, no covenant can create obligations or rights, either in the parties to it or in any person who receives power in consequence of it. All that a covenant can do, if those that make it keep it, is to alter the circumstances in which men act, so that it becomes their interest to act otherwise than they would have done without it. The political theory of Hobbes differs from that of most of the utilitarians, not because he admits the existence of natural rights and they do not, but because his theory, unlike theirs, allows of no rights at all other than legal powers. Though no one made a more frequent use of the words, 'laws of nature' and 'natural rights', it is clear that the things themselves have no place in his philosophy.

The purpose of Hobbes's sovereign is to create a harmony where none existed. The sovereign, however often he may himself disregard them or allow his favourites to do so, has the strongest interest in obliging the great majority of his subjects to obey his laws. And he has the power so to oblige them, because, though no man desires to be restrained, every other man has an interest that he should be. Thus it is that, when the sovereign forces any man to obey his laws, all other men, if they know their own interests, are his allies. The state is a society in which it is made one man's (or several men's) selfish interest to oblige every other man to behave in ways that suit his neighbours. But no man has an interest in himself obeying the laws except that his disobedience, by weakening the sovereign, makes it less likely that others will obey them. It is this, and not the flow of words about natural rights and sovereign impersonations, that is the hard core of Hobbes's political theory. It is also the doctrine that Hume, Bentham and James Mill borrow from him.

The utilitarians take little interest in the origin of the state, while Hobbes devotes many pages to its description. Hobbes is regarded as one of the great exponents of the theory of the social contract. But Hobbes's contract is unlike anyone else's. It is not a true covenant imposing real obligations on the parties to it. Hobbes, like many of the other contract theorists, does not suppose that he is describing an historical fact. The theory, for him as for them, is a convenient fiction. But its convenience lies elsewhere. His purpose is not to explain why and to what extent subjects are obliged to obey their rulers, but only to prove that it is, on all but the most rare occasions, their interest to do so. He therefore imagines a state of nature and contrasts its miseries with the comparative ease of political society. Having imagined men without government, he finds it necessary to describe the motives that could induce them to create it. But having described these motives, and introduced into his account of the institution of the sovereign a superfluous mystical element, he quietly tells us that the conqueror has the same right to rule as the sovereign established by covenant. What more could he say to prove that, in his opinion, whatever the origin of the sovereign's power, his subjects' motives for obeying him remain the same? But this is also the opinion of the utilitarians.

Hobbes, like the utilitarians after him, thought it the great function of government to reconcile selfish interests, to make it worth every man's while to obey laws giving security to all men. It is this, more than any other part of his theory, that is the essence of it, in the sense that it gives it a unity it would not otherwise possess. The state, according to him, is neither the promoter of the good life nor the protector of rights; it is the conciliator of interests. Unlike the utilitarians, Hobbes calls interests 'natural rights', and so makes it appear that, like the contract theorists before him, he regards the state as the protector of rights. Yet it is, I think, easy to see that he means no such thing, though his special use of the words 'natural rights' misleads not only his readers but sometimes also himself. For he not only calls interests rights, but applies arguments to them that could only hold if they were rights, in some sense of that word precluded by his assumptions. This is the price that anyone is liable to pay who uses words in unusual meanings.

The most important difference, in the political sphere, between Hobbes and the utilitarians, is not that he regards the state as the protector of natural rights and they do not. It is rather that his fear of anarchy leads him, against all the evidence of history, to exaggerate the need for an absolute sovereign of unquestioned authority. That he magnifies man's egoism, his vanity and his love of power matters much less, for it is by no means obvious that what he wishes us to conclude from these qualities is really made necessary by them. There can be no valid argument from human selfishness, jealousy and pugnacity to the need for unbridled government. For these qualities, though less universal than Hobbes supposes, are evenly distributed among the peoples of the world, who have known not one but many forms of stable government. From men's selfishness, vanity and need for security it is no more possible to deduce the form of government that would suit them best, than the clothes they should wear from their susceptibility to heat and cold and their love of finery. Several of the utilitarians, though they use milder language, think hardly better of mankind than does Hobbes, but not one of them is an apologist for absolute government. It is his greater fear of anarchy and not his worse opinion of his species that makes Hobbes so anxious to prove that subjects owe an almost unlimited obedience to their sovereign. Be so foolish as to challenge his authority, Hobbes tells us, and you will be plunged at once into the war of all against all.

History teaches us that Hobbes's threat is an idle one. The sovereign is strong, and the subject who dares defy him, unless he can persuade others to join him, must be a mere fugitive from justice. It is only the united strengths of many subjects that can suffice to destroy the sovereign's power. But there cannot be a union without discipline. Rebels cannot succeed unless they maintain order in their own ranks; and they cannot have security until they have made their power effective throughout the state. Those who destroy governments nearly always replace them, maintaining their power by the same means that they gained it. This is not always so. The rebels may quarrel among themselves, or there may from the first have been several claimants to the authority of the dispossessed sovereign. But the period of civil war need not last long and it may involve very little suffering for most people. Hobbes's argument is only plausible if we accept his description of the alternatives (continued obedience to the existing sovereign, and the most hideous anarchy) between which we have to choose. If we prefer to take history for our guide, we find the alternatives more difficult to assess, and it is far from obvious that submission is the wisest policy.

The utilitarians seldom look to history for political lessons. If they do not share Hobbes's preference for absolute government, it is only because they have different prejudices. Bentham and the elder Mill, for instance, were as certain as Hobbes that men ought not to trust one another. But they happened to be more afraid of misgovernment than anarchy. They therefore argued that, because men are selfish, vain, and naturally abusive of power, only a democratic government could secure them against each other's ill-usage. They accepted the opinion of Hobbes that the great function of government is to conciliate interests, and they did not quarrel with his estimate of mankind. But they did not share his fear of anarchy.

Hobbes used a traditional vocabulary unsuited to his political theory, and it was precisely this vocabulary that the utilitarians abandoned. That is why the difference between them appears so much greater than it is. But eliminate from Hobbes's statement of that theory the phrases that only serve to obscure his meaning, and what remains, except for his extravagant fear of anarchy, is strikingly similar to the fundamental political doctrines of the utilitarians.

3. LOCKE AND THE UTILITARIANS

There are some respects in which Locke, the moralist, stands closer to the utilitarians than does Hobbes. But their debt to him is much smaller. It was from the richer man that the greater sum was borrowed. And yet what was borrowed from Locke, though smaller in amount, was more easily convertible into the utilitarian currency.

Most of Locke's theory of morals, such as it is, is to be found in three chapters of his *Essay Concerning Human Understanding*.[1] By the time he has got to the last of these chapters,[2] Locke has apparently forgotten what he said in the other two. There is little that is consistent in his theory of morals; but the greater part of it resembles either the egoistic hedonism of Hobbes or the utilitarianism of a later age. His one consistent belief is that nothing is good or evil except pleasure and pain or the means to them.

Like Hobbes and the utilitarians, Locke asserts that there are no moral laws, whose validity is immediately recognized without regard to their consequences. He believes that the great variety of opinions about morals held in different societies, or in the same society at different times, are sufficient evidence that this assertion is true. 'The saints who are canonized among the Turks', he says, 'lead lives which one cannot with modesty relate.'[3] He also says that 'God, having, by an inseparable connexion, joined virtue and public happiness together, and made the practice thereof necessary to the preservation of society, and visibly beneficial to all with whom the virtuous man has to do; it is no wonder that every one should not only allow but recommend and magnify these rules to others, from whose observance of them he is sure to reap advantage to himself.'[4] That is to say, God has made it worth every man's while to behave in ways that promote the public happiness, and it is this behaviour that constitutes virtue. This is as close to the utilitarian theory of morals as Locke ever comes, and it is the doctrine that Paley borrows from him. But Locke does not, in so many words, say

[1] These are, chapter 3, of Book I; chapter 21 of Book II; and chapter 3 of Book IV.
[2] In it he says that morals is a demonstrable science, like mathematics, although he has said, in the third chapter of Book I, that there are no universally valid moral laws.
[3] *Essay Concerning Human Understanding*, Book I, chap. 3, 9.
[4] Ibid., I, 3, 9.

that the public happiness is the measure of right and wrong. He suggests that it is God who must supply men with motives for pursuing it; their object, in obeying his laws, being always their own advantage and not the public interest. There is more of egoistic hedonism than of utilitarianism in this, and yet it is a step towards the doctrine of Bentham and James Mill that Hobbes never took. Though Bentham often, and James Mill always, asserts that no man can desire any pleasure except his own, they both insist that the greatest happiness, no matter whose, is the only criterion of morality. It is this, whether or not it is consistent with their egoistic premises, that makes utilitarians of them. But Locke, like Hobbes, will have it that 'what has an aptness to produce pleasure in us is what we call good, and what is apt to produce pain in us we call evil'.[1]

There is more of the utilitarian doctrine in Locke's moral than in his political philosophy. The social contract is his central theme, and what he describes is a true covenant imposing real obligations on the parties to it. The rights that men possess in the state of nature are not, for him, mere powers, of which it would be meaningless to say that they ought or ought not to be exercised; they are powers in the exercise of which they ought to be protected by their neighbours. And it is because men have these rights and obligations in the state of nature that they can establish a ruler over them to whom they owe a duty of obedience. Their object in establishing him may be the more efficient protection of the rights on which public happiness depends, but his right to rule rests, not only on his efficient government, but much more on his subjects' consent. The conquest of power, however excellent the conqueror's government, is no sufficient title to the obedience of his subjects.

It is true that, having made consent a necessary ground of political obligation, Locke finds himself in great difficulties, and that his only way out of them is to call by that name many things that obviously are not consent. Whenever he thinks it in the public interest that men should obey their governors, he undertakes to prove that they have consented to do so. This may be, as Bentham would have suggested, an unconscious tribute to the utilitarian doctrine, but it is also evidence that it could not satisfy Locke. In chapter fourteen of the *Second Treatise of Civil Government*, Locke has an argument

[1] Ibid., II, 21.

designed to prove that when a government harms its subjects, it is acting without their consent. He thinks it obvious that people will never consent 'that anybody should rule over them for their harm.' Even at this point, when a man with not half his reputation for sagacity might have been satisfied with the utilitarian argument —that subjects have the right to revolt against rulers who harm them—Locke must bring in the notion of consent.

Locke's theories of property and of punishment, two of the greatest subjects in the domain of political philosophy, have little that is utilitarian about them. Every man is to keep the fruits of his labour because he has a natural right to them. Locke does not deny that his keeping them is in the public interest, but his title is grounded in a natural right and not in utility. Locke is a utilitarian only when he comes to explain why it is that a man may not retain more of the perishable fruits of his labour than he can consume before they spoil. Of punishment Locke tells us that by the Law of Nature every man in the State of Nature has the right to punish anyone who transgresses that Law. It is only because every man has this right in the State of Nature that a government can have it in Civil Society. We are to understand that, though punishment is useful, no government has the right to inflict it because, by so doing, it can promote the public happiness. In the political philosophy of Locke, the question of origins is always the most important. But with Hobbes its importance is more apparent than real, and all the utilitarians neglect it.

I have made a number of distinctions that some of my readers may think arbitrary. To the social contract Hobbes assigns as large a place in his political philosophy as does Locke, and yet I have said it is not as essential to it. I have also said that the utilitarians have more in common with Hobbes than with Locke, and yet the public happiness is as important to Locke as it is insignificant to Hobbes. But the public happiness as the end of government is the favourite notion of the utilitarians. Would it not have been as easy to prove that the spiritual ancestor of Bentham was Locke rather than Hobbes?

There is one concession that every writer on politics must make to the less easily satisfied of his readers. This is a subject, as Burke saw, in which there is little enough room for novelty. Or rather, novelty, if it is to be had at all, must be the fruit of patience, observation and extensive knowledge. The study of society is of all studies the least rewarding; it brings a small return on a large intellectual effort. Political thinkers have, therefore, been manipulators of ideas rather than extenders of knowledge. They had, by the seventeenth century, inherited a considerable stock of these ideas, and their originality, when it existed, consisted, as often as not, in the special uses to which they put them. This stock of ideas was not so great that an ingenious and imaginative writer could not find some place for most of them in his own system. We need not wonder, then, if we find in the political writings of Locke most of the ideas of Hobbes, except those explicitly rejected by the younger philosopher.

But this does not mean that the systems of Hobbes and Locke are not profoundly different. They are not just two varieties of the social contract theory. Locke accepts a traditional doctrine and elaborates it, so that it can serve as the theoretical justification of limited monarchy and parliamentary supremacy. The idea round which his entire political philosophy turns is that every legitimate government is the protector of rights uncreated by it and that subjects are bound to obedience only so long as their rights are protected. But the essence of Hobbes's theory is that government is the conciliator of selfish interests. If he was not the inventor of this idea, he was certainly the first modern thinker to place it at the foundation of his political philosophy. Anything unnecessary to a philosophy so grounded, though Hobbes may expatiate upon it in one place, is quietly sacrificed, should the occasion require it, in another. Thus it is that, after a long description of the institution of sovereignty, and after telling us that the subjects are the true authors of all their ruler's actions (a description not altogether unlike Rousseau's account of the General Will, and with the same air of mystery about it), Hobbes announces that conquest is as good a title as any other to government. In the last resort, all that matters with him is security or, in other words, the discipline of law under which every man finds his selfish account. To Hobbes, this discipline of law creates a harmony of interests, which is not desirable in itself though desired by every prudent man as the surest means to his own happiness. To the utilitarians, this harmony of interests is the public happiness, which is either the objective criterion of morality or else the end to which our moral sentiments are in fact directed. But this idea of government as the conciliator of interests, though Locke neither ignores nor rejects it, is not central to his philosophy. This is surely reason enough for saying that it is to Hobbes rather than Locke that the utilitarians are indebted.

CHAPTER II

HUME

1. HIS THEORY OF MORALS

DAVID HUME is rightly regarded as the founder of utilitarianism, though, like many founders, he is less uncompromising than most of his successors. He is also the inventor of a subjectivist system of ethics, which many later utilitarians adopted, either in part or as a whole, although it does not form an essential part of the doctrine. I do not mean by this that it is not an essential part of Hume's moral theory, for that it certainly is, but only that a man can be a utilitarian, in the usual meaning of the word, without adopting Hume's subjectivist system or any variety of it.

Hume does not use the word 'utilitarianism', which John Stuart Mill claims to have invented. If Mill's claim is true, the word was introduced into the English political vocabulary at about the same time as two others, both of them destined to be even more widely used and misused, namely, 'liberalism' and 'socialism'. Nor does Hume ever use the expression 'the greatest happiness of the greatest number', which is, according to F. C. Montague, to be found in the fifth edition of Hutcheson's *Enquiry into our Ideas of Beauty and Virtue*. This edition was published in 1753, six years after Hutcheson's death. But if Hume does not name the doctrine, nor invent the sacred formula, he does provide his successors with the word 'utility' of which they stand more in need than any other if they are to express their theory concisely and without ambiguity.

Leslie Stephen once said of Hume that 'the essential doctrines of Utilitarianism are stated (by him) with a clearness and consistency not to be found in any other writer of the century', and that 'from Hume to J. S. Mill, the doctrine received no substantial alteration'.[1]

It is not possible, I think, to quarrel with this verdict, provided it is understood that the 'essential doctrines' correspond, more or less, to the four criteria given at the beginning of this essay. There are many varieties of utilitarianism besides the one advocated by

[1] *History of English Thought in the Eighteenth Century*, Vol. II, p. 87.

Hume, and from the essential doctrines it is possible, if certain further assumptions are made, to draw conclusions very different from any with which Hume would have been inclined to agree.

The virtues of clarity and consistency have often been ascribed to Hume. He deserves the praise at least as much as any other important philosopher of the eighteenth century. But Hume is a careless writer; he is certainly not always consistent in his use of words, and so he sometimes gives an appearance of logical inconsistency when he is in reality perfectly aware of the implications of what he is saying. He deliberately uses the same words in different meanings, or different words in the same meaning, because he finds it convenient to do so and does not wish to appear clumsy or pedantic. Unwary readers, especially of the academic type, sometimes imagine they have caught him out when they have done nothing of the kind. Hume, like everyone who discusses difficult philosophical problems, is sometimes guilty of genuine inconsistencies, but his great defect, as a moral and political thinker, is much more often inadequacy than inconsistency. He does not take all the relevant facts into account. But even in this respect, he is greatly the superior of most of his contemporaries, and is much less inclined than they are to over-simplify.

Utilitarianism is above all a theory of morals. The political doctrines put forward by any utilitarian philosopher are no more than the conclusions he draws from his moral premises and from certain other propositions which, rightly or wrongly, he believes to be generalizations from experience. We must, therefore, first deal with Hume's theory of morals. It is to be found in the third book of his *Treatise of Human Nature*, and also in the *Enquiry Concerning the Principles of Morals*. Of these two, the latter is the more readable; but it only repeats in more elegant and less precise language what Hume had already said in the former. It will be best, therefore, to attend mostly to what he says in the *Treatise*, making only occasional references to the *Enquiry*, although Hume considered it 'incomparably the best thing' he had ever written.

Hume's ambition, as a moral philosopher, was the exact opposite of Locke's. Whereas Locke had hoped that it might one day be given to him to show that Morals is a demonstrable science, Hume's purpose, which he believed he had achieved, was to introduce the experimental method into it.

He explains to us what he thinks Ethics is in an often-quoted passage. 'The only object of reasoning' (and he means reasoning about morals) 'is to discover the circumstances on both sides which are common to these qualities' (he means the qualities that men call estimable or blameable), 'to observe that particular in which the estimable qualities agree on the one hand, and the blameable on the other; and thence to reach the foundation of ethics, and find those universal principles from which all censure or approbation is ultimately derived. As this is a question of fact, not of abstract science, we can only expect success by following the experimental method, and deducing general maxims from a comparison of particular instances.'[1]

Hume does not treat his reader to the examination of many particular instances, but passes almost immediately to his conclusions. 'Morals', he says, 'excite passions, and produce or prevent actions. Reason of itself is impotent in this particular. The rules of morality, therefore, are not conclusions of our reason.' '. . . Reason . . . can have an influence on our conduct only after two ways: Either when it excites a passion by informing us of the existence of something which is a proper object of it; or when it discovers the connexion of causes and effects, so as to afford us the means of exciting any passion.'[3] Hume means that it is not reason but our emotions that prescribe the ends we are to pursue. We can, according to him, no more expect reason to prescribe to us what we ought to desire for its own sake than to determine what we do desire. We must, of course, use our reason in order to understand what sort of creatures we are and how our behaviour is in fact determined; but there are no things, good or evil in themselves, or actions, right or wrong in themselves, whose moral qualities are independent of our own attitude to them and which we can but recognize. Hume invites the reader to examine any action usually called vicious. 'Wilful murder, for instance; examine it in all lights, and see if you can find that matter of fact or real existence which you call vice. In whichever way you take it, you find only passions, motives, volitions and thoughts. . . . The vice entirely escapes you, as long as you consider the object. You never can find it, till you

---

[1] *Enquiry Concerning the Principles of Morals*, Sec. 1, § 5.
[2] *Tr. H. Nat.*, Bk. III, Pt. 1, Sec. 1, p. 457 (Selby-Bigge edition, Oxford, 1896).
[3] Ibid., III, 1, 1, p. 459.

turn your reflection into your own breast, and find a sentiment of disapprobation, which arises in you, towards this action.'[1] His conclusion is that 'an action or sentiment, or character is virtuous or vicious . . . because its view causes a pleasure or uneasiness of a particular kind'.[2] Things are good and bad, therefore, because the contemplation of them causes pleasure or displeasure to the persons who observe them or who think about them; and this pleasure or displeasure is always of a particular kind, which Hume does not define (though he does not say it is indefinable) but which he considers to be the same thing as approval and disapproval.

Hume altogether rejects egoistic hedonism. He says that we do not approve or disapprove of characters and actions because they are or are not beneficial to ourselves. He says: 'The good qualities of an enemy are hurtful to us; but may still command our esteem or respect. 'Tis only when a character is considered in general, without reference to our particular interest, that it causes such a feeling or sentiment, as denominates it morally good or evil'.[3] The dismay that we feel when someone does what will injure us, or our violent delight when we receive a great benefit, must not, according to Hume, be confused with disapproval and approval. These two latter sentiments are, as he is never tired of telling us, always disinterested. Even when someone is good to us, we can distinguish between our approval of his benevolence and our pleasure at the good done to us. Both these sentiments are pleasant, but they are quite different from each other. Had our benefactor been equally good to someone else, we would, presumably, have felt the former sentiment but not the latter.

Hume is a careless writer. His words sometimes imply that we approve or disapprove of an action or a character whenever the contemplation of it causes us pleasure or pain. At other times, he speaks of pleasure or pain of a certain kind; and it is then clear that he has come nearer to his real meaning. But the phrase 'pleasure or pain of a certain kind' is ambiguous. When we say that we distinguish between kinds of pleasure, we may mean only between kinds of pleasant things or between pleasures having different causes, without suggesting that they are pleasant in different ways; or we may mean that we distinguish (if that is possible) between kinds of pleasure in the same way as we distinguish between colours.

[1] Ibid., pp. 468-9.   [2] Ibid., p. 471.   [3] Ibid., p. 472.

C

Hume's meaning is not clear. He often speaks as if approval and disapproval were particular kinds of pleasure and pain, but his words also suggest that there are only differences of degree between different pleasures and different pains, the peculiarity of approval and disapproval consisting only in this, that they are pleasure and pain caused by the disinterested contemplation of a character or an action. By 'disinterested contemplation' no more is meant than contemplation unaffected by any hope of benefit or fear of injury likely to accrue to the contemplator or to any person to whom he is not indifferent. Hume is right in believing that we can contemplate in this way actions that benefit or injure ourselves. We can, as it were, consider our own predicament as if it were anyone else's.

It is probable that Hume means by approval and disapproval, not a special kind of pleasure or pain, but a pleasure or pain caused in a particular way. Yet this is an interpretation on which it would be a mistake to insist, not only because no one can be certain what Hume does mean, but also because it is likely that, whatever he means, he is wrong. Approval and disapproval are emotions, while pleasure and pain are not, but are merely qualities that emotions or feelings sometimes possess. Moreover, approval can be unpleasant and disapproval pleasant. Indeed, in the countries of Northern Europe and North America, disapproval is a favourite form of self-indulgence.

The reader may have noticed, from the passages so far quoted, that Hume does not distinguish between good and right, or between evil and wrong. A state of mind, a motive or a disposition of the character is good or evil because we approve or disapprove of it; and an action is right or wrong for exactly the same reasons. As for the obligatoriness of an action, it consists, in Hume's opinion, in nothing more than the fact that the thought of not performing it, when we are able to do so, causes us displeasure of the kind which is disapproval. Thus obligatoriness and rightness are not, for Hume, the same thing. When I approve the performance of an action, I call it right; when I disapprove the non-performance of it I say that the prospective agent, whether myself or somebody else, is under an obligation to perform it. And when the action is one that I could myself perform, then my disapproval of the non-performance of it is a motive for performing it. That is to say, it is an emotion which might cause me to perform it, and in fact always would cause me to do so if there were not other motives operating in the contrary direction.

So much, then, for Hume's views about good and evil and right and wrong. The reader will observe that nothing yet said about him is a reason for considering Hume a utilitarian. Though most utilitarians have shared many or at least some of the opinions of Hume so far discussed, they are none of them essential parts of the utilitarian doctrine. We cannot say that because Hume has these opinions he is a hedonist; all that we can say is that, if he is a hedonist, he cannot be an egoistic one after the manner of Hobbes. We can also say that, if he is a hedonist, he is a utilitarian; but we must first establish that he is a hedonist.

Now it is clear that Hume is not a simple hedonist, such as Hobbes and Bentham always were, and Locke sometimes. He nowhere asserts that nothing is good except pleasure and nothing evil except pain. All that he does say is that men usually approve or disapprove whatever, in the society in which they live, is either pleasant or a means to pleasure, or else is painful or a means to pain. This, he would have us believe, is a fact about human nature that we can do nothing but accept. It is by observation of human behaviour, and in no other way, that we come to know it. Hume does not equate pleasure and goodness, nor does he claim to apprehend any necessary connexion between them. That the two are connected is, he thinks, vouched for by our experience. It is one of those generalizations that their author says are empirical though he produces no evidence to support the assertion.

It is easy to see that Hume does not equate pleasure and goodness. He says that men usually approve, not only what is pleasant, but what is a means to pleasure. But it is clear that the means to pleasure (for instance, a virtuous action requiring great courage) may be very painful. Hume, therefore, must believe that we can approve of what is very painful; from which it follows that what is very painful may be good. And observe that Hume does not assert, what Bentham did assert, that what is painful may be a means to the good but must itself be evil. On Hume's theory, what is a means to pleasure can be just as good as what is pleasant; for all that is required for a thing to be good is that the disinterested contemplation of it should normally arouse pleasure. Hume is explicitly committed to the view that we approve the means to pleasure as much as pleasure itself; and therefore that many other things besides pleasure are good. If a hedonist is defined as a person who maintains that only pleasure is good, and if utilitarianism is treated as a variety of hedonism, then it is clear that Hume is not a utilitarian. Whoever does not wish to come to the absurd conclusion, that the founder of utilitarianism is not a utilitarian, will take good care to define the doctrine in such a way as not to be obliged to do so.

Hume's utilitarianism consists, therefore, in this: that he maintains that men normally approve of those states of mind or actions that are pleasant or a means to pleasure, and disapprove of those that are painful or a means to pain, no matter whose the pleasure or pain. It is the primary importance he attaches to pleasure and pain, his opinion that a pleasure or pain, no matter whose, is as good or evil as any other equal to it, that make him a utilitarian. He says: 'Every quality of the mind is denominated virtuous, which gives pleasure by the mere survey; as every quality, which produces pain, is call'd vicious. This pleasure and this pain may arise from four different sources. For we reap a pleasure from the view of a character, which is naturally fitted to be useful to others, or to the person himself, or which is agreeable to others, or to the person himself. One may, perhaps,' Hume goes on, 'be surpriz'd, that amidst all these interests and pleasures, we should forget our own, which touch us so nearly on every other occasion. But we shall easily satisfy ourselves on this head, when we consider, that every particular person's pleasure and interest being different, 'tis impossible men cou'd ever agree in their sentiments and judgments, unless they chose some common point of view. . . . Now, in judging of characters, the only interest or pleasure, which appears the same to every spectator, is that of the person himself, whose character is being examined; or that of persons who have a connexion with him.'[1] This, if it means anything, means that the moral sentiments are disinterested; and it also means that they are shared, though felt more intensely by some than by others, by all or nearly all men.

Hume, then, is a utilitarian but he is not a complete one. He thinks that the characters and actions approved or disapproved by nearly all men are for the most part those that usually promote pleasure or pain. But he is not sure that this is so always. He says

[1] *Treatise*, p. 591.

'. . . these sentiments' (he means approval and disapproval) 'may
arise either from the mere . . . appearance of characters and
passions, or from reflexion on their tendency to the happiness of
mankind . . . My opinion is that both these causes are intermix'd
in our judgments of morals. . . . Tho' I am also of opinion, that
reflexions on the tendencies of actions have by far the greatest
influence, and determine all the great lines of duty.'[1]

This passage is interesting, not only because it shows us that
Hume is not a complete utilitarian, but also because of the great
importance it ascribes to reason. Hume goes so far as to say that
reflexions on the tendencies of actions determine all the great lines
of duty. But he does not usually ascribe as much importance to
reason as he does in this passage. It is experience that teaches us
which actions usually have pleasant consequences and which have
painful ones; and learning from experience involves the use of
reason. But Hume does not mean that we must each of us come to
the conclusion that a certain type of action is usually productive of
pleasure before we come to approve it. His view is rather that we
imitate, in this respect, the fashions prevalent in the society in which
we live. All of us most of the time, and many of us all the time,
approve and disapprove from mere habit, without worrying our
heads about the probable consequences of the actions approved or
disapproved. But these habits are themselves, over long periods
of time, directed by the 'collective' experience of mankind or of the
society in which we live. It is, so Hume believes, a law of human
nature that men will never long approve what injures them or
disapprove what causes them to be happy.

Hume lived in a society more stable, in many respects, than our
own. I do not mean that it was less liable to disorder, but merely
that it changed more slowly. Scotland, Hume's native land, did,
of course, change rapidly during the eighteenth century, but only
to become more like England than she had been before. The
standards of behaviour prevalent in his own day among the
educated classes of Western Europe seemed to Hume to be fairly
stable; and he quite simply assumed that conformity to them would
lead, on the whole, to as much happiness and as little unhappiness
as men could reasonably expect. He did not consider the case of a
rapidly changing society, in which men's habits, formed in an earlier

[1] Ibid., pp. 589–90.

age, no longer suit the one in which they live. In such a society, men might approve of many things, formerly beneficial but now injurious, and disapprove of others, formerly injurious but now beneficial. Since, according to Hume, it takes time to form the habits that direct the moral sentiments, it must always be true that, in a rapidly changing society, the prevailing moral standards will never promote the greatest happiness possible.

No theory of morals assigns a larger role to sympathy than does Hume's. Hume explicitly rejects the notion that egoism is in any sense fundamental, and altruism either a disguised form of it or else its derivative. In rejecting Hobbes's psychological hedonism, he borrows the simple argument of Bishop Butler, that a man must be able to desire other things besides his own pleasure, because, before anything can please him, he must first desire it. A man must, before he can get pleasure from quenching his thirst, feel thirsty. And if he can desire other things besides his own pleasure, there is no reason why other people's pleasures should not be among those things. Egoistic hedonism is usually of the psychological kind. It is not absurd to hold that, though men can desire pleasures not their own, it is their own pleasures that they should strive to obtain. But few people have ever been tempted to accept this theory, which, though it is logically impregnable, is far less plausible than the one adopted by Hobbes. What Butler and Hume, therefore, most desire to do is to refute Hobbes. For the egoistic hedonism of Hobbes is not properly a theory of morals. It does not explain the facts of our moral experience but obliges us to reject them as illusions. Hume is as well aware as anyone, and much better aware than either Bentham or James Mill, that no true moral philosophy can make an accommodation with Hobbes.

Hume defines sympathy as the pleasure or pain we feel whenever we contemplate the pleasures or pains of other people. And from sympathy springs benevolence; because the pleasure of other people gives us pleasure, we wish to give pleasure to them, and because the pain of other people gives us pain, we wish to relieve them. This, of course, is not to reduce benevolence to egoism. We do not desire to give pleasure to other people in order that their pleasure should give us pleasure; on the contrary, our own pleasure, so far from being the object of our desire, is merely the cause of it. There is no trace of Hobbesian egoism in what Hume has to say about sympathy and benevolence.

Having established its right to an existence independent of egoism, Hume is anxious not to make too much of sympathy, for all that it must play so important a part in his system. Our sympathy, he says, is seldom intense, except when the pleasures and pains of those to whom we are most closely bound by blood or friendship are concerned. Sympathy is a weak emotion on most occasions when we feel it and the benevolent impulses aroused by it are usually much weaker than our selfish passions.

But though sympathy is a weak emotion, it is one to which we are all liable. Human souls are so much alike that no sooner does one man approach another than the bonds of sympathy are established between them. Though they may not like one another, they will not, unless they are mere passers-by, be indifferent. This does not mean that Hume would deny that we are indifferent to many people whom we see or hear during the course of the day, for we may know nothing of them. But if we converse with any of them, however small our interest, we cannot listen to what they say about themselves without some faint sympathy or antipathy. If this much is admitted, Hume thinks it enough for his purpose, which is to prove that the moral sentiments, though strong enough to control the behaviour of all mankind, are yet derived from sympathy.

Hume puts the gist of his argument into a short passage in which he says: '. . . tho' sympathy be much fainter than our concern for ourselves, and a sympathy with persons remote from us much fainter than that with persons near and contiguous; yet we neglect all these differences in our calm judgments. . . . Besides, that we ourselves often change our situation . . ., we every day meet with persons, who are in a different situation from ourselves and who cou'd never converse with us on any reasonable terms, were we to remain constantly in that situation and point of view, which is peculiar to us. The intercourse of sentiments . . . makes us form some general unalterable standard, by which we may approve or disapprove of characters and manners. And tho' the heart does not always take part in those general notions . . . yet they are sufficient for discourse, and serve all our purposes in company, in the pulpit, on the theatre, and in the schools.'[1]

It is easy to see how Hume distinguishes between sympathy and the moral sentiments. Sympathy is the pleasure or pain we feel when we contemplate the pleasures or pains of other people. The moral sentiments are the pleasures and pains we feel when we contemplate actions or characters without regard to any benefit or injury that may result from them to ourselves or to persons in whom we take a special interest. Sympathy and the moral sentiments have different objects; they are aroused in us by the contemplation of different things. Moreover, the moral sentiments are disinterested, while sympathy is not. But though the distinction between them is clear enough, it is difficult to see how Hume derives the moral sentiments from sympathy. How does an emotion that is strong only when persons close to us are involved give rise to sentiments that are completely disinterested? Hume sees the difficulty and often refers to it, but not every one will agree that he has solved it. What are the calm judgments in which we neglect all the differences in sympathy so natural to us? They are presumably judgments about the consequences of human actions and characters. We may, for instance, reasonably conclude that a crime committed in China two thousand years ago caused as much unhappiness as one committed yesterday in our neighbourhood and involving our closest friends in hopeless misery. In the one case we feel only the faintest sympathy, and in the other our hearts go out to our friends. If our feelings of disapproval in the two cases are equal, or at least much nearer equal than our feelings of sympathy, how is it that the former are derived from the latter? Our calm judgments can, perhaps, explain how it is that we disapprove the two crimes equally, but they cannot make more intelligible the derivation of the moral sentiments from sympathy. It is not enough to say with Hume that the one class of feelings derives from the other, to admit the greatest differences in the operations of the two and to say that these differences are accounted for by the influence of our calm judgments. Why should not our calm judgments level our sympathies as effectively as our moral sentiments? There may well be a causal connexion between the two kinds of feelings; indeed, it is likely

[1] *Treatise of Human Nature*, pp. 603–4.

that there is. But then each kind is causally connected with many other things as well, so that our knowledge is not much extended by saying that one is derived from the other. Hume's derivation of the moral sentiments from sympathy is no more plausible than James Mill's derivation of them from egoism.

Hume's words suggest that sympathy and the moral sentiments, though they have different objects, are similar feelings. He says that when a man calls another his enemy, he speaks the language of self-love and expresses sentiments peculiar to himself. But if he calls him vicious, he speaks another language and 'expresses sentiments, in which he expects all his audience to concur with him. He must here, therefore, depart from his private and particular situation . . .; he must . . . touch a string to which all mankind have an accord or symphony.'[1] There is nothing here that implies that the sentiments expressed differ in kind, and the most natural interpretation of Hume's meaning is that they are similar, though in the one case the man who expresses them knows they are peculiar to himself, while in the other he expects his hearers to share them. But to most people approval and disapproval seem to be emotions very different from sympathy and antipathy. This is a matter that introspection alone can decide. Nor will most persons agree with Hume when he says that approval and disapproval are weak sentiments. He may never have felt them strongly, but then he was a very exceptional person.

In a passage to which he attaches little importance, Hume reveals his greatest defect as a moral philosopher. He discusses the distinction made by modern philosophers (but not by the ancients) between the natural abilities and the moral virtues. He admits that the quality of our approval of the natural abilities differs from the quality of our approval of the moral virtues. Yet both the abilities and the virtues are beneficial to mankind or immediately agreeable to those who possess or contemplate them. Hume explains the difference between the qualities of our reactions to these two classes of phenomena by the circumstance that, whereas the natural abilities are largely unalterable, the virtues, or at least the actions proceeding from them, can be stimulated by rewards and punishments, by praise and by blame. All this is certainly true. What is curious is that Hume should treat it as if it were unimportant, whereas it is, in fact,

[1] *Enquiry*, Sec. 11, Part 1.

whatever its correct analysis, of the essence of the matter, and of it
every adequate theory of morals must take large account.

Before we can profitably discuss Hume's political philosophy, we
must notice a distinction he makes between the natural and the
artificial virtues. The natural virtues, such as courage, prudence
and benevolence, are the products of natural instincts; and every one
readily understands both that they are so and that they are beneficial.
Prudence and courage are necessary for self-preservation, and
benevolence, the product of sympathy, obviously increases human
happiness. But there are other virtues which, in Hume's words,
'produce . . . approbation by means of an artifice or contrivance,
which arises from the circumstances and necessity of mankind'.[1]
He regards justice as a conventional virtue of this kind.

Now, when Hume talks of justice, he means, above all, respect for
the existing conventions about property. It is easy to see why these
conventions are respected once they are established, for, in every
society, thieves, when caught, are punished. What needs explanation is how it is that such conventions come to be established.
They are not the immediate products of any natural instinct.
It is true that men are benevolent, but benevolence, according to
Hume, though it cannot be explained away or derived from
egoism, is normally much weaker than men's selfish passions.
It cannot therefore explain how the conventions about property
first arose. Nor, of course (though Hume does not bother to make
this point), could the conventions about property and the respect
for them be imposed by the strong upon the weak. For it is the
inequality of property which itself divides society into the strong and
the weak. The conventions about property must therefore precede
the inequality that makes possible the domination of the many by
the few. The question, therefore, still remains: how did these conventions arise?

Hume's answer is that 'nature provides a remedy in the judgment
or understanding, for what is irregular and incommodious in the
affections. For when men . . . have observ'd, that the principal
disturbance in society arises from those goods, which we call
external, and from their looseness and easy transition from one
person to another; they must seek for a remedy . . . This can be
done after no other manner, than by a convention enter'd into by

[1] *Treatise*, p. 472.

all the members of the society to bestow stability on the possession of those external goods, and leave every one in the peaceable enjoyment of what he may acquire by his fortune or industry.'[1] In this passage, as he himself points out, Hume is not using the word convention in the sense of contract. 'It is only,' he says, 'a general sense of the common interest . . . which induces them to regulate their conduct by certain rules. . . . In like manner are human languages gradually establish'd by human conventions without any promise.'[2] Hume, a little later, puts his main argument in these words: ' 'Tis certain that no affection of the human mind has both sufficient force, and a proper direction to counterbalance the love of gain, and render men fit members of society, by making them abstain from the possessions of others. Benevolence to strangers is too weak for the purpose. . . . There is no passion, therefore, capable of controlling the interested affection' (Hume means 'love of gain') 'but the very affection itself, by an alteration of its direction. Now this alteration must necessarily take place upon the least reflexion; since 'tis evident that the passion is much better satisfy'd by its restraint, than by its liberty. . . .'[3]

Whenever nature provides us with anything we need in sufficient abundance, we evolve no conventions regulating its use. Property is the product of selfishness, scarcity and reflexion. Now, once the conventions have come into existence, it is obviously convenient, in the long run, that they should be respected even in those cases where respect for them creates unhappiness; for mankind have more to gain by their general observance than to lose by their observance in hard cases. It may sometimes be in the public interest that the conventions should be altered, though Hume takes no notice of this point; but it can almost never, he is careful to insist, be in the public interest that they should be broken. Hume's account of the origins of justice and property is very different from Locke's; he has nothing to say about man's natural right to the product of his own labour. So far, then, Hume's account is much closer to that of Hobbes than to any one else's. But all that he has yet done is to explain how certain conventions and the respect for them have come into existence; he has not yet explained why this respect is a virtue. This last, however, is the easiest part of his task. Though self-interest was the original motive that led to the establishment of

[1] Ibid. p. 489.   [2] Ibid., p. 490.   [3] Ibid., p. 492.

justice, it is sympathy with the public interest that is the source of the moral approval that attends its practice.

All that Hume has established, if his arguments are valid, is that it is in the public interest that there should be some rules of property; but he has not given us reasons for believing that the rules prevailing in any society are more likely to be in the public interest than other rules which could be devised to take their place. He might have argued that, since men must learn by reflexion that some rules are necessary, this same process of reflexion enables them to discover what rules are best suited to their needs. But Hume does not do this. He merely says that '. . . there are, no doubt, motives of public interest for most of the rules which determine property; but I still suspect, that these rules are principally fix'd by the imagination.'[1] He then goes on to explain how the imagination does the fixing; how 'first possession always engages the attention most'; how, when first possession becomes obscure through the passage of time, 'long possession or prescription takes its place, and gives a person a sufficient property in anything he enjoys'; how a natural association of ideas leads us to suppose that what belongs to a father should, after his death, belong to his son. The imagination, according to Hume, is largely governed by the laws of the association of ideas. How then can he think it probable that the rules of property fixed by the imagination are the rules which, on the whole, best promote the public interest? Hume merely makes an assumption and leaves it at that. The weakness of his argument, at this point, is typical of him; it lies not in any confusion of thought or logical inconsistency but in a simple failure to take all the relevant circumstances into account. It was left to Hume's successors to justify or to condemn the existing laws of property on strictly utilitarian grounds.

Hume has only one argument for the inequality of wealth. It is an argument often used for want of a better. Create equality of possessions among men, and their different abilities will soon restore inequality. Or if the equality is forcibly maintained, society is reduced to indigence, for its ablest members have nothing to induce them to make the most of their abilities. The argument implies that equal possessions mean equality of poverty, and that no egalitarian society can be rich. Hume, like most people who use it,

[1] Ibid., Note to p. 504.

does not care to determine just how much inequality it justifies. It is an argument for no more than unequal rewards for unequal labour, and it does not justify any system of property existing in the world. But Hume, living in a society in which only the inarticulate had important grievances, did not give, and did not need to give, thought to such matters.

Another conventional virtue, to which Hume also devotes much attention, and which he considers to be part of justice, is the keeping of promises.[1] Hume's argument to prove its conventional nature does not differ, in any important respect, from what he has to say about property. A man's mere statement about how he intends to act on a future occasion can, of itself, impose no obligation on him, for it cannot provide him with any motive for doing in the future what he now says he intends to do. It is human conventions that create such a motive, for they are the products of an experience teaching us that human affairs are conducted to better advantage, when every man has some security that every other man will do what he says he intends to do. To this end, there are established certain forms of words among men, by which they can give each other this security. These forms once established, whoever uses them 'must never expect to be trusted any more, if he refuse to perform what he promis'd'.

I have given a mere outline of Hume's moral theory, whose details are no longer of great interest. It reduces morals to a branch of psychology; and it is this that is its principal defect in the eyes of many people. With this common verdict, the reader may or may not agree. Whatever the defects of the theory, it is as subtle and plausible as any other system of ethics propounded by a European between the times of Aristotle and Kant. The reader will have observed that it owes almost nothing to Locke, and a great deal to Hobbes. But it is very different from Hobbes's theory, and includes an explicit rejection of much that Hobbes taught. The influence of Hobbes on Hume is as much negative as positive, but it is incomparably greater than that of any other thinker.

Hume's theory, usually in a cruder form than the one given to it by its inventor, dominated English moral philosophy until it began to be affected, well on into the nineteenth century, by the system of Kant. Even Bentham and James Mill, who taught that the standard

[1] He sometimes calls this virtue 'fidelity'.

of morality is independent of men's sentiments, had perforce to borrow several arguments from Hume to show how it is that men come to accept that standard. James Mill, though he derived them both from egoism, made a large use of sympathy and approval to explain the moral behaviour of man. Though many persons attacked Hume, nearly all of them who undertook to construct a moral theory of their own incorporated a considerable part of his with it. And they borrowed very little from Kant, who was heard of in this country long before he was understood. But it was widely known that many of Kant's arguments were directed against Hume, some of whose critics seem to have sheltered under the authority of a name that was still only a name to them. Sir Leslie Stephen, who had the patience to read many of Hume's critics, gives the impression that some of the attacks on him were made with weapons believed by their users to have been borrowed from Kant, though it is now known that they were made in Scotland by the very people who thought they had imported them from Germany.

Yet it would be a mistake to suggest that nearly all utilitarians adopted or else adapted to their own use Hume's theory of morals. Many of them were not moral philosophers and were content to assert that only pleasure and the means to pleasure are good, and that no action is right except the one likely to produce the greatest happiness under the circumstances. They did not attempt to analyse the notions of goodness and rightness or to explain man's moral behaviour. But those utilitarians who went at all deeply into these matters, though they might explicitly reject some part of Hume's teaching, usually borrowed at least as much as they rejected.

2. HIS POLITICAL THEORY

Hume's political theory is simpler than his ethics, and what originality it has is mostly negative. It is what he rejects rather than what he adds to the ideas current in his day that distinguishes him from his predecessors. He does not talk of natural law and natural rights, and he quietly demolishes the notion of a social contract. Otherwise, except for a few favourite ideas of his own which all his historical studies failed to dislodge from his mind, he follows Hobbes.

Hume's moral theory rests on the psychological assumptions that sympathy is not a form of egoism and that the moral sentiments are a species of sympathy. But his political theory takes it for granted that man is predominantly selfish and often foolish. It is, he thinks, 'a just political maxim, that every man must be supposed a knave: though at the same time, it appears somewhat strange, that a maxim should be true in politics, which is false in fact.'[1] Men are truly benevolent in the circle of their families and friends, but their benevolence is too weak to have a larger operation. Besides, in their political behaviour men are partisans, and their selfishness is therefore less liable to restraint. Those whose interests are the same will applaud them whatever they do, and this applause will make them indifferent to the opinions of others. Lonely and unsupported man is, Hume implies, easily influenced and restrained by the opinions of other men, but as soon as he acquires a circle of friends he has shelter and comfort against the rest of the world and can even enjoy its hostility. This, I take it, is what Hume means when he says that honour is a powerful restraint on individual man in his dealings with other men but not on the partisan in his dealings with groups to which he does not belong.

Justice and stable government are advantageous to man; he has intelligence enough to know it but not the wisdom to act accordingly. He often prefers the immediate advantage to be gained from injustice to the more lasting but less obvious advantages that are the fruits of a constant respect for justice. How, Hume asks, is this misfortune to be remedied? His answer is that 'this infirmity of human nature becomes a remedy to itself, and that we provide against our negligence about remote objects, merely because we are naturally inclin'd to that negligence'.[2] As men cannot change their natures, the most they can do is to alter the circumstances under which they act, and so provide themselves with motives for behaving justly when they might otherwise not do so. But this can be done only in one way, by making a few men immediately interested in the maintenance of justice and giving them the power to enforce it. These few men are the civil magistrates, who, since they are indifferent to the great majority of those they govern, have no interest in doing injustice to them, but do have an interest in seeing that they act justly to one another, since the existence of the state and their own pre-eminent position inside it both depend upon the

[1] *Essay*, VI, 'On the Independence of Parliament'.   [2] *Treatise*, p. 536.

maintenance of justice. 'Here then,' says Hume, 'is the origin of civil government and society . . . Men are not able radically to cure . . . that narrowness of soul, which makes them prefer the present to the remote . . . All they can do is to change their situation, and render the observance of justice the immediate interest of some particular persons . . .'[1] This is substantially the doctrine of Hobbes. The initial assumptions are the same, though they are somewhat qualified: men are predominantly selfish, they are capable of reflexion, and they are passionate and foolish. And the conclusion is not very different: men must, for their own sakes, guard against their own and other people's rapacity and folly, and this they can do only by bringing into existence a new situation, in which they make it some powerful persons' immediate interest to force them to act in their own permanent interests, even when it is to their immediate advantage to do otherwise.

This view, as it is expounded by Hume, does not imply any particular theory about the historical origins of the state, whereas it forms part of Hobbes's account of those origins. But otherwise there is little enough difference between them. It is Hume's opinion that civil government probably first arose because, in time of war, some one man acquired an ascendancy over the others, who soon got used to discipline and felt the advantage of it.[2] All government is, he says, based on opinion. Force is always with the governed, and in the last resort the few can govern the many only because the many feel, however obscurely, that it is to their advantage to be governed.

It is not Hume's doctrine that it is 'on opinion only that government is founded',[3] that distinguishes him from Hobbes. Hobbes's account of the contract and of the sovereign as the bearer of his subjects' wills is a piece of mysticism that contains no element of truth, but in another sense his theory attaches as much importance to opinion as does Hume's. However reluctant any man may be to obey the laws when he stands to gain by disobedience, all other men are of opinion that he should obey; and it is their opinion that makes it possible for the government to enforce obedience with considerable economy and efficiency. Hobbes is even more conscious than Hume of the weakness of governments, and no less

---

[1] *Treatise*, p. 537.   [2] *Essay*, V, 'Of the Origins of Government'.
[3] *Essay*, IV, 'Of the First Principles of Government'.

convinced that their efficiency depends upon the opinion of the governed that they are indispensable. If Hobbes makes much more than does Hume of fear of punishment as a motive for obedience, it is because he thinks that reasonable people can have no sufficient motive for obeying the government unless they are convinced that the unreasonable will be bound to a similar obedience. But the first law of nature, from which Hobbes derives all the others and therefore also the obligation to obey the government, is just the sort of prudential maxim to which Hume alludes when he says that all government is founded on opinion.

Where Hume does differ from Hobbes is in the importance he attaches to the mere force of habit. He distinguishes between opinion of interest and opinion of right. The first is what we have been discussing already, the prevalent (though not, perhaps, explicitly held) opinion that government is indispensable. The second is mere prejudice created by habit, the opinion that those who have long received obedience are entitled to receive it. This, too, need not be a conscious opinion; it may be and often is no more than deference to those who speak with authority. Opinion of right maintains not only the power of governments but also the security of property. Hume thinks that the hope of private advantage (as distinct from the protection that every man enjoys where the laws are properly enforced), fear and affection contribute but little to the stability of governments. Whenever he can do it, without placing a new burden on men's virtues, Hume shifts the emphasis away from the calculating egoism, the vanity and the fear in terms of which Hobbes delights to explain the political behaviour of mankind. What belongs neither to virtue nor to vice can easily be ascribed to habit and to the association of ideas. The political importance of prejudice is a notion which both Burke and the later utilitarians owe to David Hume.

Hume's belief that government is necessary, that men have an implicit idea of its utility, and that this idea, as a motive for obedience, is powerfully reinforced by mere habit and prejudice, leads him quite naturally to the conservative conclusion that it is best to submit quietly to whatever government we find established in the country in which we live. Habit and prejudice are strongest where society has changed the least. There is therefore a presumption against change and a very strong presumption against violent

D

change. In the most important of his political essays, *Of the Original Contract*, Hume says that though some innovations must take place, violent ones are to be undertaken by no individual and are dangerous even when attempted by the legislature. Men must expect more evil than good from them, for though there are examples to the contrary, 'they are not to be drawn into precedent, and are only to be regarded as proofs, that the science of politics affords few rules, which will not admit of some exception, and which may not be sometimes controlled by fortune and accident'.[1] Hume speaks of 'violent' innovations but we may take it that he means great ones, for he says that they are dangerous even when the legislature attempts them, and what is done by the legislature is presumably peaceably done. This is the conservative doctrine of the man who was not only the least orthodox of the great English philosophers but also a life-long student of history.

There is another argument, from which Burke and Bentham were to derive conservative consequences, to be found in Hume. It is that stability of property is to be maintained, not only to prevent disputes, but also so as not to disappoint the expectations which it has created. 'By the laws of society', says Hume, 'this coat, this house is mine, and ought to remain perpetually in my possession. I reckon on the secure enjoyment of it; by depriving me of it, you disappoint my expectations, and doubly displease me, and offend every bystander.'[2] From this simple argument many consequences can be and indeed often have been drawn. Men are creatures of habit, and habits create expectations. It is therefore important, if men are to be happy, that they should be able to enjoy in the future what they have enjoyed in the past and are enjoying in the present. To deprive them of their property is to deprive them of the means to expected future enjoyments. But to disappoint expectations that are the creatures of habits, is to destroy those habits, and therefore to weaken the bonds that hold society together. Besides, men suffer more from being deprived of what they have long possessed than other men are made happy by being given what they never expected to have. There is a *prima facie* case against all transfers of property. What all men want is security; and though, if there is insecurity, some may gain what

---

[1] *Essay*, XII, 'Of the Original Contract'.
[2] *Enquiry Concerning the Principles of Morals*, Appendix III.

others lose, they not only gain less than others lose but they cannot be secure in its possession, for the stability of property, on which security depends, has already been shaken for their benefit.

These consequences, suggested or implied by Hume and later developed by Burke and Bentham, are impressive only in isolation. As soon as we call to mind the law of diminishing utility and also the fact that the spoliation of the rich has prevented bloodshed perhaps as often as it has occasioned it, we can estimate Hume's argument at its true value. Arguments *a priori* are nowhere more out of place than in political theory, but it is precisely in this sphere that even the most sceptical of philosophers does not abandon them. He calls his preferences generalizations from experience and he laughs at the intuitionists, but the foundations on which he builds are no stronger.

Hume, indeed, in matters political was no true sceptic. He was a man of calm temper and quiet prejudices. He disliked confusion of thought and empty symbols, but, provided a statement was meaningful, clear and plausible, he was not much disturbed by lack of evidence for its truth. The genuine scepticism of Montaigne, the true freedom from prejudice which is not a kind of intellectual nihilism but is the product of sympathy and imagination, was not his.

Hume's greatest service as a political theorist is his indifference to questions of origin. As an historian he is, of course, as interested in them as anyone else, but he does not wish to draw political conclusions from them. No matter how governments came into existence, the present duty of obedience is always grounded in utility. 'If the reason be asked of that obedience, which we are bound to pay to government, I readily answer, because society could not otherwise subsist. And this answer is clear and intelligible to all mankind. Your answer is', he says to the contract theorist, 'because we should keep our word. But besides, that nobody, till trained in a philosophical system, can either comprehend or relish this answer: Besides this, I say, you find yourself embarrassed, when it is asked, why are we bound to keep our word? Nor can you give any answer, but what would, immediately, without any circuit, have accounted for our obligation to allegiance.'[1] In other words, fidelity, or the duty to keep promises, is as much grounded in

[1] *Essay*, XII, 'Of the Original Contract'.

utility as any other duty. Why, then, derive the duty of obedience from it, when it can be more directly and plausibly derived from utility? Since we have no knowledge of an original contract and much evidence that existing governments acquired their power by force and fraud, is it not wiser to abandon an intricate theory that is difficult to understand and still more difficult to defend? And if we do so, we can also abandon all such obscure notions as that of 'tacit consent', which are only invented to support a theory whose weakness is felt by its own exponents. These arguments, made to look less simple, are to be found once again in Bentham's *Fragment on Government*. There they are used as a base for a hundred unkind attacks on Sir William Blackstone. But Hume is seldom aggressive; he is content to point out errors and to invite his readers to pass another way.

There are two classes of important political thinkers: those whose fertile minds produce many ideas for later generations to elaborate, and the spell-binders. Hume, like Aristotle, belongs to the former class, though he occupies a humbler place in it. It is the measure of Plato's greatness that he not only belongs to both but is first in each of them.

CHAPTER III

FROM HUME TO BENTHAM

FOR a period of over a hundred years, utilitarianism was the dominant political and moral theory in England. This period lasted from the time that Hume's reputation as a philosopher was made until the publication of J. S. Mill's essay in defence of a doctrine that he had himself, without knowing it, more than half rejected. I do not wish to say that all or even most of the writers on politics and morals were utilitarians. The dominance of a theory, unless it is a creed maintained by a church or a state, does not ordinarily involve its explicit adoption by any large number of those who write or think about the subject with which it deals. The utilitarians, properly so called, were always a minority. Their theories were not flattering to mankind and were therefore repeatedly attacked. Something of the unpopularity of Hobbes, from whom they derived so many of their ideas, always remained with them.

But though the utilitarians were always on the defensive, either to recommend themselves to the world or to expose the follies of their critics, they also produced most of the theories and ideas around which political and moral discussion turned. Their vocabulary, their turns of speech, their favourite prejudices, and their hatred of nonsense served not only their own purposes but often those of their opponents as well. They were aggressive and self-confident, and always ready to do battle provided the ground were chosen by themselves. For they were sure that, on any other ground, the battle must be unprofitable to all the combatants; it must be a mere war of words. Complacency and their sort of scepticism are natural allies, and they make a formidable combination. Formidable, indeed, but not attractive; and that is why the utilitarian doctrine has always been more influential than popular. When the effects of their actions need not be considered, even fanatics are less annoying than the sceptics who, whatever else they may doubt, are always sure of their own wisdom. And it is the religious who search their hearts. In their devotion to their creed there is often a true humility,

and we are moved to respect them even when we know the harm
they do.

But the doctrine's very great influence is what nobody can deny.
For over a hundred years, the moral and political philosophers of
England and Scotland did little more than either elaborate the
theories of Hume and of Hobbes (the latter in the more respectable
form given them by Hume), or else protest against them and
construct the weakest alternatives. The great contemporaries
whose theories (if only small though important parts of them
are true) destroy utilitarianism at its roots were all foreigners.
Rousseau, Kant, Saint-Simon and Marx were unknown or mere
names in England until the late nineteenth and early twentieth
centuries. Rousseau had made too great a reputation in the world
to be ignored even by the English, but he was also held responsible
for inspiring a revolution. The English therefore condemned his
doctrines, discovered a good deal of nonsense in them and took no
notice of the rest. Those who had heard of Kant spoke of him
respectfully. It was well known that his heart was in the right place,
and that on all important questions he was on the side of the angels.
But his theories were complicated and his language obscure.
Here was a great piece of artillery indeed and the utilitarians used
only muskets, but unfortunately there was as yet no one in England
who could handle so large a gun. Saint-Simon died in 1825 and
Marx only in 1883. They were both original thinkers and very
shrewd and severe critics of the societies in which they lived.
Time was therefore needed for the intellectual world to get used to
them and to recognize their importance.

Thus it was that the utilitarians, for over a century, had no
serious competitors. They could even afford not to make use of all
the advantages provided by the subtlety of Hume. As we shall
see, Bentham and James Mill impoverished more than they en-
riched the doctrine inherited from him. There are some people,
often hard-working and virtuous, who feel uncomfortable except
in narrow and barely-furnished rooms.

Nothing, however, would be less just than to accuse all the
utilitarians of austerity. When a doctrine becomes dominant, it
acquires some of the virtues of the society it dominates. Richness
and variety are characteristic of all the great nations of Western
Europe, and of none more than England. The fundamental utili-

tarian assumptions were made, either openly or tacitly, by many men whose theories have little more than these assumptions in common. It was the fashion, in politics and morals, to erect tall structures on slender foundations. Philosophical systems are artificial things, and philosophers who begin with the same assumptions can arrive at the most different conclusions. His fundamental principles, if he is unable to invent them, a moralist may borrow from others, but the system he derives from them will depend upon his experience and his character.

I shall therefore, though I deal only with the most important, have something to say not only about Helvetius and Beccaria, but also about Paley, Burke, Godwin, Paine, Adam Smith, Malthus and Ricardo. All these men, who were among the cleverest thinkers of their day, were indebted either to Hume or Bentham, or to both of them.

Bentham started out on his intellectual career with only a small stock of ideas. These he took mostly from Hume, but also from Helvetius, Beccaria and Priestley. When Bentham, after an undergraduate career at Queen's College, which he thought a waste of time, revisited Oxford in 1768 to record his vote at the University Parliamentary election, he found, in a little circulating library attached to Harper's coffee-house near his old college, a copy of a pamphlet which had only very recently been published, Priestley's *Essay on Government*. In this pamphlet, he found the magic phrase 'the greatest happiness of the greatest number'. If, then, Bentham got no wisdom at Queen's College, he got the piece of it that he valued most very close at hand. He records his experience in these words: 'It was by that pamphlet and this phrase in it that my principles on the subject of morality, public and private, were determined. It was from that pamphlet and that page of it that I drew the phrase, the words and the import of which have been so widely diffused over the civilized world.' The phrase, however, though Bentham found it in Priestley's pamphlet, was not the invention of Priestley. Sir Leslie Stephen, Professor Halévy and Dr. Montague agree in ascribing the authorship to Francis Hutcheson.

1. HELVETIUS

Neither Priestley nor Hutcheson is of great importance in the history of moral and political thought; certainly of much less importance than Helvetius and Beccaria. Helvetius, who lived from 1715 to 1771, was the Frenchman who did more than any other man to make popular Hume's philosophy on the Continent. His book, *De L'Esprit* (1758), is an attempt to analyse all human experience into sensations, by which he means exactly what Hume meant by impressions and ideas. It is, with Hartley's *Observations on Man*, Condillac's *Traité des Sensations*, and James Mill's *Analysis of the Phenomena of the Human Mind*, one of the four most ambitious and systematic attempts to work out in detail the implications of Hume's general principles. But Helvetius's more complicated and less subtle gallicized version of Hume's theory of knowledge does not concern us. We are concerned only with two doctrines of Helvetius, of which one was borrowed from Hume and the other is more closely associated with Helvetius himself. Both these doctrines are much older than the eighteenth century, but it was because Helvetius brought them together and attached great importance to them that they later fired the imagination of Bentham. The first of these doctrines, borrowed from Hume but on which Helvetius leant much more heavily than his master had done, is that the chief utility of governments consists in their ability to force men to act in their own best interests when they feel disinclined to do so. This doctrine, expounded with the greatest clarity and force in Hobbes's *Leviathan*, has been called the principle of the artificial identity of interests. In his most interesting but often misleading book, *The Growth of Philosophic Radicalism*, M. Halévy compares this principle with two others, which also assume the predominant selfishness of men: the principle of the fusion of interests and the principle of their natural identity. The former asserts that, though men's selfishness of itself leads to conflicts between them, its operation is to some extent counteracted by that of sympathy. The latter asserts that though each man seeks his own selfish interest, the world is so made that he can only do so by co-operating in peace and amity with other men. The most famous exponent of what Halévy calls the natural identity of interests is Bernard Mandeville, whose book *The Fable of the Bees* was published in 1714. Mandeville gave his book the sub-title *Private Vices, Public Benefits*, and he succeeded in giving it an appearance of paradox by assuming that most natural passions, and especially the pursuit of wealth, are vicious, and then going on to prove that they are necessary to civilized life. The core of Mandeville's argument is that while every want is an evil, it is the multitude of men's wants that obliges them to serve one another and therefore to live in peace and amity; from which it follows that the greater and more varied men's wants, the more their selfish desire to satisfy them will oblige them to co-operate in the production and distribution of the goods by which alone these wants can be satisfied. This argument, divorced from its author's paradoxes, is easily recognized as the most important of the assumptions made by the classical economists. What Mandeville did for the principle of the natural identity of interests, Helvetius did for that of their artificial identity. He did not invent it, but he made the most of it.

The other idea of Helvetius, also not original with him, but to which he ascribed no less importance, is that man's character is entirely the product of his environment. He seems to have imagined that this is a legitimate inference from the phenomenalism he took over from Hume. But Helvetius did not agree with Montesquieu that national character is largely determined by a people's climatic and geographical environment. He thought man's social environment a more important factor in making him what he is than the geography of his country. Now, whereas geography and climate are beyond human control, social environment is not. Man, by acquiring knowledge of what he is and what made him so, acquires an almost unlimited power to reform his species. But there are in society two classes of persons who can do more than any others to reform their fellows; they are the pedagogues and the legislators. It is their business to give men the education and the laws that will enable them to attain happiness. In the eyes of Helvetius, the pedagogue and the legislator co-operate in the same task; they are both of them primarily educators. Divorced from its phenomenalist origins and its utilitarian bias, this doctrine of Helvetius, that good laws make good men, is as old as Plato and Aristotle. But at the time that he expounded it, men were struck by its novelty. In any case, it is an idea not to be found in Hume. But what is still more important to notice is its essential radicalism. The three Englishmen who were the most completely converted to it, Bentham, Godwin and

Robert Owen, were among the most radical critics of the society
in which they lived.

2. BECCARIA

The doctrine of Helvetius that morals and legislation, well considered, are the same science, was taken up by the Italian philosopher
Beccaria, whose book *Dei delitti e delle pene* (*Of Crimes and Punishments*) first appeared in 1764. It is an attractive and well-written
book, and it quickly attained the greatest popularity. It contains
the first Italian version of the famous utilitarian phrase, in the words
'la massima felicità divisa nel maggior numero'. 'If we look into
history', says Beccaria in an often-quoted passage from the introduction to his book, 'we shall find that laws, which are or ought to
be conventions between men in a state of freedom, have been for the
most part the work of the passions of the few or the consequences of
fortuitous or temporary necessity; not dictated by a cool examiner
of human nature, who . . . had this only end in view, the greatest
happiness of the greatest number.' Beccaria, like Bentham after
him, proposed to make the scale of punishments correspond to the
scale of crimes. One of his rules was that punishments should always
be so contrived that, with the least possible pain to the culprit,
they should produce the greatest deterrent effect; another, that
punishment should be certain and immediate; yet another, that
judges should never interpret but should confine themselves to
applying the law. These are but three principles, among many,
which Bentham was to take directly from Beccaria. But whereas
the Italian philosopher merely put forward a number of principles
which he did not elaborate, the Englishman corrected them, added
to them, and derived innumerable consequences from them.

Helvetius and Beccaria were undoubtedly, after Hume, the two
greatest influences on Bentham's intellectual life. Bentham, as we
shall see later, was not primarily a moral or political philosopher.
What he has to say to us about the nature of goodness and obligation, law, society and government, is neither new nor ingenious.
Indeed, his moral philosophy, such as it is, is so confused and
ambiguous as to be scarcely deserving serious study. In this respect,
he is not merely greatly inferior to Hume, but is not even the equal
of his own disciple, James Mill. He has been compared with a good
mathematician who has the most confused notions about the

philosophy of mathematics, and who can perform the most complicated operations without being able to define such notions as 'number', 'class' and 'function'. Most mathematicians put up with this deficiency with a good grace, knowing that their calculations will be none the less accurate on account of it. But Bentham was not so easily satisfied, and he involved himself in difficulties of whose exact nature he was not even aware. His real virtues are those of the codifier of law and the technical reformer; and the importance of Helvetius and Beccaria to him is that they showed him the road on which he was to travel.

3. PALEY

Before the world had heard of Bentham, another utilitarian philosopher had made a great reputation. I mean William Paley, whose account of a utilitarian God promoting the happiness of his entirely selfish human creatures, was intended to reconcile Englishmen inclined to philosophy with the religion by law established in their country. Paley is so much the disciple of Hobbes that his doctrine, strictly interpreted, may appear hardly to deserve to be called utilitarian. He is as much an egoistic hedonist as any man ever was. And yet it would, I think, be a mistake to deny him the name of utilitarian. Bentham himself often uses the language of egoistic hedonism; and so, too, does James Mill, and much more consistently than his master. Nevertheless, these three writers all try to reconcile their egoistic hedonism with the fashionable utilitarian doctrine, that that action is right which leads to the greatest possible happiness, no matter whose. The difference between Paley, on the one hand, and Bentham and the elder Mill, on the other, is that Paley's reconciliation is more mechanical and less plausible. It may be that the cause of virtue is further from his heart; that having, like James Mill, derived benevolence and morality from the selfish passions, he is more ready to keep their origins constantly in view. It is for this reason only that Paley, rather than Bentham or James Mill, deserves to be called a pseudo-utilitarian. Fear plays as great a part in his system as in that of Hobbes.

It is in God that Paley finds the conciliator of egoism and utilitarianism. Though Paley believes that every man desires only his own happiness and can desire no other man's except as a means to his own, he also believes that God desires the greatest happiness of the greatest number of men. Paley's God is the one true utilitarian in the universe, for He desires men's greatest happiness for its own sake. That the happiness of God should depend upon that of His creatures is a maxim that no clergyman will advance, so that Paley, unlike Hobbes, does, after all, ascribe an immense importance to genuine altruism. Though the greatest happiness of the greatest number is desired for its own sake by only one person, that person happens to be omnipotent. He can therefore easily contrive that His creatures shall desire it as a means to their salvation.

No utilitarian, not even Hume, is more conservative than Paley. There are traces of utilitarianism in Burke, who is as conservative as Paley, but his apology for prevailing conditions is much less explicitly utilitarian. Burke was the more emotional and imaginative of the two men, and unlike the philosophic clergyman he was religious by nature. Paley is too brisk and confident when he explains God's business in the world. Could any man, who felt his own weakness and mortality, speak so familiarly of One whom he believed to be his Maker? Men have stood in greater awe of their employers than this clergyman of his God.

Paley's *Principles of Moral and Political Philosophy* appeared in 1786. 'Moral Philosophy,' he tells us, is 'that science which teaches men their duty and the reasons for it.'[1] He believes that when men have noticed that the conduct of other men is beneficial to themselves, a sentiment of approval arises in their minds, and afterwards accompanies the idea or mention of the same conduct, although the private advantage that first excited it no longer exists. Beneficial, for Paley, means productive of happiness, and happiness is but the excess of pleasure over pain. 'Pleasures', he says, 'differ in nothing, but in continuance and intensity.'[2] So far, all that Paley has said is perfectly compatible with utilitarianism, for though he has told us that we begin by approving only what is beneficial to ourselves, this does not exclude the possibility that we later approve what is beneficial to others. For the sort of conduct that benefits one man usually benefits another. If, then, we continue to approve it after the private advantage that first excited it no longer exists, we may well approve it when the advantage is someone else's. Paley, however, indifferent to the implications of what he has said, will not allow that man is charitable. He defines virtue as 'the doing of good

[1] *Principles of Moral and Political Philosophy*, Vol. I, p. 1.   [2] Ibid., p. 21.

to mankind, in obedience to the will of God, and for the sake of everlasting happiness'.[1] He asks his readers the question 'Why am I obliged to keep my word?' 'Because it is right, says one.—Because it is agreeable to the fitness of things, says another.—Because it is conformable to reason and nature, says a third.—Because it is conformable to truth, says a fourth.—Because it promotes the public good, says a fifth.—Because it is required by the will of God, concludes a sixth.'[2]

Paley's conclusion is that all these answers are right, because 'the fitness of things, means their fitness to produce happiness: the nature of things, means the actual constitution of the world, by which some things . . . produce happiness, and others misery: reason is the principle, by which we discover . . .this constitution: truth is this judgment expressed or drawn out into propositions, . . . and such . . . is the divine character, that what promotes the general happiness is required by the will of God; . . .'[3] It can be seen from this quotation that Paley was a man of the world. He tells the adherents of these rival doctrines that they are all right, and leaves it to them to infer that he is himself more right than them all. Bentham would have proceeded in a different fashion: he would have said that all the others were wrong and he alone was right.

But Paley is aware that he has still left the matter short. He has told us that right means 'conforming with the will of God', but he has not told us why we are obliged to do what is right. His final answer to the question, 'Why am I obliged to keep my word?' is, therefore, that 'I am urged by a violent motive resulting from the command of another'.[4] The violent motive is the expectation of a posthumous reward, and the command is God's. 'Private happiness is our motive, and the will of God our rule.'[5] It is our good fortune that we live in a world in which man, the incurable egoist, has everything to fear and everything to gain from a just, omnipotent and benevolent God.

Paley is nothing if not positive. He justifies his conservatism by two arguments, of which one is that 'happiness is pretty equally distributed among the different orders of civil society', and the other, that 'the advantages of property are so great that men are willing to tolerate the greatest inequalities provided it is respected'.

[1] Ibid., p. 41. [2] Ibid., p. 54. [3] Ibid., p. 55. [4] Ibid., p. 59.
[5] Ibid., p. 60.

He has a little parable in which ninety-nine strong and healthy men toil all day for a poor wage to produce a heap of superfluities to be spent or spoiled by a feeble and worthless man, by a child, a woman, a madman or a fool. They look quietly on while the fruits of their labour are consumed, but should one of their number touch or take the least particle of these superfluities, the others would set upon him and hang him for a thief. This picture is not quite true to life, if only because there is no judge or executioner brought into it to hang the wrong-doer, but it is the fruit of Paley's imagination. He looks upon it with complacency and reflects that the benefits of property must indeed be great if men will behave in this way.

In considering the nature of civil government, Paley insists on the fact that the governed are many and their governors few. The physical strength, he concludes, resides with the governed. The question which therefore lies at the root of all political speculation is this: What are the motives that induce the many to submit to the few? No single motive, says Paley, is sufficient; but there are three altogether more important than the rest. The first, and most important, is *prejudice*, which Paley defines as 'the opinion of right founded on custom', i.e. the prevalent opinion that those persons who have long exercised a power have the right to do so. Hume expresses the same idea when he says, in the *Treatise of Human Nature*, that most men, if asked whether they had ever promised to obey their rulers, would think strangely of their questioner and would reply that they were born to such obedience. The second motive is *reason*, or the reflexion, of which only a minority are capable, that government is necessary for human welfare and that it entails obedience. The third motive is *self-interest*, which does not so much attach men to their governments as detach them from combinations against them. Absorbed in their own affairs, men find it difficult to co-operate against their governors. Since prejudice is the main source of a government's authority, it follows that 'every innovation in the constitution, or, in other words, in the custom of governing, diminishes the stability of government.'[1] But Paley does admit that it might sometimes be expedient to use force to get rid of one's rulers, and he approves of the Revolution of 1688.

[1] Ibid., Vol. II, p. 126.

In his criticism of the notion of a social contract and of natural rights, except in the sense of rights that men might still possess outside politically organized society, Paley is a typical utilitarian. But what is more interesting is that he uses his utilitarian principles as the major premises of arguments to prove that the system of parliamentary representation existing before the Great Reform Bill was perfect; that judge-made law (i.e. the binding force of judicial precedents) is good; that the old English penal laws, which hanged a man for stealing a sheep as well as for murder, were excellent; that a very great inequality of wealth is beneficial to the community; and that a religious establishment is desirable. His argument for the inequality of wealth is typical of him. One of the most effective ways of increasing happiness is, he thinks, to increase the number of people who can be happy. It is therefore desirable that the population should increase.[1] But the wealthy, marrying later than the poor, have fewer children; on the other hand, Paley is convinced that one class of society are about as happy as another. It is therefore desirable that most people should be poor. Why, then, need any be rich? Paley's answer is that a small proportion of the population of a country can produce all the necessaries required by the whole of it. But this small proportion will produce only enough for themselves, if they have no inducement to do otherwise. The others must provide this inducement by offering them luxuries in return for their necessaries. This is as far as Paley cares to take his argument, but it has consequences that may well have been clear to him. One such consequence is that it cannot be desirable that all the producers of necessaries should receive luxuries in return for them; for in that case a large minority of the people would be wealthy enough to marry late and have small families. It is therefore proper to infer, from what Paley says, that that society is best organized in which most of the producers of necessaries are poor, and the recipients of luxuries are only a small class of land-owners and capitalists. For Paley is just as insistent that idleness leads to vice and unhappiness as he is that poverty does not. Paley, in fact, logical though he is, does not carry his argument to its logical conclusion. He justifies inequality; but he does not say, what on his own

---

[1] Paley believed that most countries, Britain among them, could easily support much greater populations than existed in his day.

premises he should say, that the greater the inequality the better for mankind.

I have devoted some considerable space to Paley for two reasons: because of his great influence while he lived, and also because he is in some respects so like and in others so unlike Bentham. From theoretical principles that are broadly similar, except that Bentham says nothing about God and often speaks as if the greatest happiness of the greatest number were desirable in itself and not because some one omnipotent person desires it, Paley and Bentham arrive, on nearly all practical questions, at very different conclusions. Nor are these differences due to the fact that Paley was a clergyman and Bentham was not. Had Paley been an atheist, and even a pure utilitarian and not an egoistic hedonist as well, he might have arrived at the same conclusions. Like every other fashionable doctrine, utilitarianism can be adapted to suit a great variety of temperaments.

4. BURKE

Paley was much more of a utilitarian than Burke. It would, perhaps, be less misleading to say that, whereas Paley made a deliberate effort to reconcile his religious beliefs and his conviction of the absolute selfishness of men with utilitarianism, Burke made no such attempt to systematize his ideas. Whereas Paley was consistently at least a pseudo-utilitarian, Burke sometimes came close to being a genuine one.

The utilitarian bias in Burke, as Halévy has shown in his book on *Philosophic Radicalism*, is exhibited in three ways. The gist of his argument against any except the most careful and moderate reforms, is that an institution's having lasted a long time is itself a proof of its utility, of its conduciveness to human happiness. There are, he argues, forces that tend to disrupt every human institution: disintegration and decay are facts that nobody will deny. If, then, an institution has lasted a long time, it has resisted these disruptive forces and has thereby proved its utility.

The utilitarian bias is also evident in Burke's argument in favour of prescription. One of the most lively sentiments in every man is expectation. Now, every man expects to keep what he has; and the longer he has had it, the keener his disappointment at its loss. Moreover, this expectation is normally stronger than the hope of obtaining something not possessed before. From these premises, Burke arrives at his conclusion that long possession, or prescription, is 'the most solid of all titles, not only to property, but, which is to secure that property, to Government'.

The second of these arguments is to be found in Hume; and even the first is implicit in much that he says. But Hume does not lend particular emphasis to either. As for Burke's third utilitarian argument, in favour of prejudice, it has the same origin as his second. No one knew better than Hume that we must take an immense number of opinions on trust, and that the longest life and the most perceptive mind can enable their possessor to justify or to repudiate only a few of them. Apart from the most necessary of all prejudices, the belief in causality, for which, says Hume, there can, from the nature of the case, be no evidence, there are a host of others, many of them verifiable in principle, but which no reasonable man would refuse as guides to action before he had verified them. There is, nevertheless, an important difference of opinion between Hume and Burke in the matter of prejudice. Hume does, no doubt, agree that many of the opinions we accept on trust can be verified, but his words often suggest that there are others, no less useful, whose truth or falsity can never be established. When he speaks of religion, Hume is careful not to give offence, but there can be little doubt that among men's religious beliefs he would find many useful but unverifiable prejudices. There are some beliefs without which men cannot live at all, and others without which they cannot live happily. Their minds need shelter and comfort no less than their bodies, or the world will be too much for them.

Burke's attitude differs from Hume's in two respects. He thinks that all the great prejudices on which the stability of human societies depends are capable of verification. They can be shown to be true, and they are useful and give comfort only because they are true. The fundamental moral laws and religious doctrines have been so long the possession of mankind that no good purpose can be served by their criticism, since it is impossible to improve upon them or to add to their number. There is no trace either of cynicism or scepticism in what Burke says about morality and religion. But he not only believes that there is no room for improvements in morality and religion, but also that it is dangerous to put this matter to the test. Societies in which first principles are too often examined

E

and may be rejected by every arrogant fool who thinks himself wiser than the rest of mankind are in danger of dissolution. It is not by prejudice alone, but by reverence and humility as well, that men can live in society. This is an attitude that takes us far indeed from Hume, and it explains the deep influence of Burke on such Catholic thinkers as de Maistre and de Bonald.

Burke was not primarily a utilitarian; but in so far as he was one, he was closer to Hume than to any other representative of the school. He did not share Hume's ultimate scepticism, and he was as unlike him as an Irishman can be unlike a Scot; but he borrowed some of his most striking arguments and put them to uses of which Hume might have approved, though he would have taken them more coolly than did Burke. Burke's political theory is also like Hume's in not being set out in propositions, precise and unqualified, which are treated (whatever their authors may say about them) as if they were self-evident. There is a largeness of view about both Burke and Hume, which is not to be found in the writings of Bentham, Paley and James Mill. No doubt, the principles on which Bentham and the elder Mill rest their political and moral theories are supposed by them to be generalizations from experience. But little or no evidence is offered for their truth, and the reader is expected, in practice, to take them as self-evident. Burke and Hume also make unfounded assumptions, but these form part of philosophies that embody a much wider experience. Nor do they, like Bentham and James Mill, place these assumptions simply and squarely at the foundations and then build the most rigid systems upon them.

CHAPTER IV

JEREMY BENTHAM

1. HIS LIFE AND INFLUENCE

WE now come to the man who, if he did little to establish the principles on which the utilitarian philosophy rests, is certainly, in the opinion of most men, the most typical utilitarian of them all. Jeremy Bentham applied utilitarian principles to the discussion of a great variety of political, legal and administrative problems with a thoroughness unrivalled by anyone else. It is no wonder that he was the first utilitarian to have disciples, and to create something that deserves to be called a school of thought. He was not so much a moral and political philosopher as he was a theoretical reformer. It was he who devised some of the best arguments in favour of many of the most important reforms undertaken in this country during the nineteenth century. He did for utilitarianism what Sidney and Beatrice Webb were later to do for British socialism; but he was, if I may say so without disrespect, intellectually superior to the Webbs. If the reader is sometimes astonished by the ease with which Bentham arrives at his first principles, by his confident neglect of difficulties, psychological and philosophical, of which he seems scarcely to be aware, and by the confusions and ambiguities of which he is so often guilty when discussing first principles, he cannot but admire the extraordinary clarity and vigour with which he applies those principles to the most difficult and intricate technical questions. There are several intellectual virtues that Bentham lacked, but he was completely the master of those he possessed. To his readers he still gives the impression of an exceptionally vigorous intellect.

Bentham was born in 1748 and died in 1832. In spite of some years wasted in Oxford, he had the good fortune, very early in life, to discover the principles which were to guide his intellectual activities during the rest of it. It was, as we have seen, in 1768 that he came across the formula 'the greatest happiness of the greatest number'. He seems to have had no doubts, thereafter,

59

about what he should do with his life or the utility of what he was doing. Happy, hard-working, benevolent, unimaginative and unmarried, with a mild affection for music, animals and friends, he had nothing to distract him, and he was able to devote an exceptionally long life to the development of his theories. Bentham was quite aware that he had taken his first principles from other men; his primary task was to establish the methods by which they could be applied in practice. In Leslie Stephen's words, 'In Bentham's mind, the difference between this' (i.e. the science of method he wished to establish) 'and the more general formula' (i.e. the greatest happiness of the greatest number) 'was like the difference between the statement that the planets gravitate round the sun, and the more precise statement that the law of gravitation varies inversely as the square of the distance'.[1] His primary task was therefore to discover to what extent and in what way accurate quantitative comparisons of different sums, or 'lots', of happiness could be made. But he was not to confine himself to this task; he was also, throughout his life, to criticize existing institutions and to describe the reforms that would make them as productive of happiness as possible. Bentham devoted most of his time to these secondary tasks; and what he had to say about them has proved of more permanent value to mankind than his account of how lots of happiness can be measured and compared. Nor did Bentham first deal with his primary task and then go on to the others; he did whatever work he thought it most expedient to do at the time, but he never lost sight of his scheme as a whole. Nor, of course, did he regard what I have called his primary task as more important than the others; on the contrary, he undertook it for the sake of the others.

Bentham's first published work was the *Fragment on Government*, which appeared in 1776. This book, about which I shall have more to say later when I deal more specifically with Bentham's theories, is an attack on Blackstone and on the Whig notion of a social compact of which Blackstone was an equally hesitant critic and defender. His *Fragment on Government* brought Bentham to the notice of Lord Shelburne, who sought him out in 1781. Bentham was, for a time, a frequent visitor of Shelburne's at Bowood, where he met Camden, Dunning and Pitt, and above all Dumont, the Genevan who was to do so much to popularize his theories on the Continent. Though

[1] Leslie Stephen, *The English Utilitarians*, Vol. I, p. 179.

Bentham had first met him elsewhere, it was also at Bowood in 1788 that he acquired the friendship of Romilly. Dumont and Romilly may be said to have been Bentham's first disciples.

Bentham's brother Samuel had gone to Russia in 1780, and in 1783 had been sent by Prince Potëmkin to supervise an industrial establishment at Kritchev on the Dnieper. Jeremy left England in August 1785 to stay with his brother, and did not return to this country until February, 1788. It was while he was in Russia that he wrote his *Defence of Usury*, in which he argued that Adam Smith should never, on his own principles, have condemned it. It was also while Bentham was in Russia that Paley, in 1786, brought out his *Principles of Moral and Political Philosophy*. Bentham's friends, seeing that Paley had already expressed many ideas which they knew Bentham shared, urged him to return to England and to establish a great literary reputation in his own language. It was in 1789 that Bentham at last published his *Introduction to the Principles of Morals and Legislation*, his most important philosophical work, in which he laid down the principles he intended should guide him in all his future work.

The French Revolution failed to excite or to disturb Bentham. He laughed at the principles put forward by the revolutionaries to justify their actions. He thought them fallacious, but, unlike Burke, he was not at all sure they were pernicious. He was surprised that people should take seriously the arguments advanced for and against the French Revolution by Paine and Burke, for he was equally contemptuous of Paine's logic and Burke's sentimentality. Bentham was, however, always willing to give good advice. Already in 1788 he had prepared, for the benefit of the French Estates due to meet early the next year, his *Essai sur la Représentation*, in which he advised the French to look to American models. He advocated manhood suffrage (or, at least, a very low property qualification), and also secret voting. But Bentham was not yet a convinced democrat. He knew, however, that many of the French were democrats, and he was anxious to inform them how they could best carry out their principles. In 1789, Bentham produced his *Essay on Political Tactics*, which he sent to the Abbé Morrelet for the benefit of the French Assembly. This essay was politely received, but the advice it contained was not taken. In it, Bentham inquired into the manner in which a deliberative assembly ought to conduct its business if it is to do so efficiently. Bentham's conclusions are derived from his study of British parliamentary practice, and the *Essay* is altogether an admirable example of his work. It is the first really important study on legislative procedure, and Bentham said of the English system which he analysed, that 'in this bye-corner, an observing eye may see the original seed-plot of English liberty: it is in this hitherto neglected spot that the seeds of that invaluable production have germinated and grown up to their present maturity, scarce noticed by the husbandman, and unsuspected by the destroyer'. We now know that, as early as the fifteenth century, the English Parliament conducted its business on quite different principles from those of the French Estates; that it had already become a much more efficient governmental instrument than any of its Continental counterparts. It is to Bentham's credit that he was perhaps the first person to see clearly and to explain what this efficiency consisted in.

In 1790, Bentham produced a third work for the benefit of the French, his *Draught of a Code for the Organisation of the Judicial Establishment in France.* In this work, he criticized a draft proposed by a Committee of the National Assembly, and suggested alterations, many of which are distinctly democratic in character. But Bentham was still not a convert to democracy. It was rather as if he were saying to the French legislators: 'You are democrats. I therefore invite you to be true to your principles, and I, for one, will be interested in the result'. He was interested in the French Revolution as some people were, between the two World Wars, in what has sometimes been called the 'Russian experiment'. As a reward for his good advice, in August 1792, Bentham, along with Paine, Priestley, Mackintosh and Wilberforce, was made a French citizen. Although he was almost as well disposed to the French as Hume had been, he did not set great store by this honour.

It was not the French Revolution but a succession of English Tory governments that converted Bentham to democracy. Indeed, after the massacres of September 1792, Bentham lost interest in France, and he devoted the better part of his energies to a scheme for the erection of a model prison, the *Panopticon.* As early as 1794 his scheme was officially sanctioned by Act of Parliament, but it was not until 1799 that a suitable site was obtained at Millbank, by which time Bentham had already spent several thousands of pounds inherited from his father. Nothing, however, came of the scheme; and in 1811 a committee reported against it on the ground that Bentham and his brother were to make profits from the criminals' labour. The committee agreed that Jeremy and Samuel were men of unimpeachable character, but argued that their successors might not resemble them. In 1813, Bentham received £23,000 as compensation for the final rejection of a scheme originally sanctioned by Act of Parliament, and on which he had spent large sums of money. His experiences in this matter converted Bentham to democracy. He asked himself how it was that a scheme, so obviously excellent and in the public interest, could come to be rejected. It became clear to him that those in authority had not the public interest at heart, and that they were indifferent to it because they were not truly the agents of the public.

Until 1802, Bentham was comparatively unknown. In that year, Dumont published in Paris his *Traités de Législation Civile et Pénale*, compiled from manuscripts given to him by Bentham. Dumont was an excellent interpreter of Bentham's meaning, and his work was free from the digressions and over-elaborate arguments in which his master delighted. The publication of this work made Bentham's reputation on the Continent and in America, and it was not long before he became equally famous in his own country. In 1809, Dumont was invited to Russia to prepare a Code of Law on Benthamite principles; in 1817, he was performing the same service for his native Geneva; while in 1821 the Portuguese Parliament invited Bentham himself to prepare an 'all-comprehensive' code. A year later he put before the world his *Codification Proposal*, in which he offered to prepare a code of law for any nation in need of a legislator. To this proposal Bentham appended his testimonials. Meanwhile, he continued until his death his life-long labour, his enormous and unfinished *Constitutional Code*. Bentham enjoyed his great reputation and was fully aware that he deserved it. According to Leslie Stephen, 'he is said to have expressed the wish that he could awaken once in a century to contemplate the prospect of a world gradually adopting his principles and so making steady progress in happiness and wisdom'.[1]

Meanwhile, in 1808, Bentham had met James Mill, and it was James Mill who, more than any other man, helped Bentham to

[1] Leslie Stephen, *The English Utilitarians*, Vol. I, p. 230.

draw democratic inferences from his unfortunate experience over the *Panopticon*: Bentham's *Catechism of Parliamentary Reform*, published in 1809, was the first of his several writings in defence of democratic principles. In it he advocated most of the reforms that became the common stock of English Radicalism in the first half of the nineteenth century. Other men had written in favour of these reforms long before Bentham took it upon himself to do so, but the arguments advanced by them had not been strictly utilitarian in character and had involved appeals to principles (e.g. natural rights) that were plain nonsense in the eyes of Bentham. As the apologist of reform, Bentham was in his element. He could discover more and better arguments than anyone else and could illustrate them with great vigour.

2. THE *Fragment on Government*

Two of Bentham's better-known works deal with questions that belong properly to the spheres of political and moral philosophy. They are the *Fragment on Government* and the *Introduction to the Principles of Morals and Legislation*. They are, perhaps, the most readable of his writings, though they do not illustrate his powers as well as do some of his more technical discourses.

The *Fragment on Government* was designed by Bentham as an attack on a small part of the Introduction to Blackstone's *Commentaries*, in which Blackstone offers some general definitions. Bentham quotes selected passages from Blackstone and subjects them to a meticulous examination. His criticisms are often trivial and unfair; and it is not in them that the modern reader is likely to be interested but rather in what Bentham has to say for himself.

Already, in the preface, Bentham gives expression to his most cherished conviction that 'it is the greatest happiness of the greatest number that is the measure of right and wrong'.[1] He then goes on to give evidence of his reforming zeal, objecting to Blackstone's 'ungenerous antipathy' to reform, which of itself seems 'to promise a general vein of obscure and crooked reasoning'. Bentham is confident that there is an intimate connexion between some of the gifts of the understanding and some of the affections of the heart. Bentham, indeed, was an ardent reformer and a lover of mankind for nearly forty years before he became a democrat.

[1] *Fragment on Government*, p. 93. (Edition with Introduction by F. C. Montague.)

Bentham next goes on to argue that the principle of utility, which Blackstone entirely neglected, gives us the best criterion for classifying the 'elements of jurisprudence'. He says that 'the mischievousness of a bad law would be detected . . . by the difficulty of finding a place for it in such a [natural] arrangement, while, on the other hand, a technical arrangement' (Bentham means the sort of classification offered by Blackstone) 'is a sink that with equal facility will swallow any garbage that is thrown into it'.[1] In other words, classify the laws according to a rational principle, and the very process will teach you what existing laws ought to be abolished or amended and what new laws made. Hence one reason for the great importance that Bentham attached throughout his life to the codification of law. The other reason was his belief that a logically arranged code of clearly expressed laws must be intelligible to the layman, and so decrease the powers of judges, solicitors and barristers, whose sinister interest it is to maintain a complicated and obscure system, intelligible to none but themselves. But the sinister interests of the class of men whom Bentham often referred to as 'Judge and Co.' are not made much of in the *Fragment on Government*.

Bentham's definition of the state or political society is one that most later utilitarians have adopted. Bentham tells us that 'When a number of persons (whom we may style subjects) are supposed to be in the habit of paying obedience to a person, or an assemblage of persons, of a known and certain description (whom we may call governor or governors) such persons altogether (subjects and governors) are said to be in a state of political society'[2] . . . This definition is very close to, and is indeed the model of, the famous one subsequently offered by Austin in his *Lectures on Jurisprudence*. Bentham, however, did not share the precise and rigid views about government and sovereignty that we associate with the name of Austin. The habit of obedience might be more or less perfect, and Bentham did not pretend to know what degree of perfection was required before the society in which it existed might properly be called a state. Bentham, unlike Austin, does not assert that in every State there must be some person or set of persons whose powers are legally unlimited; he merely says that, unless the powers of the governors are expressly limited by convention, it is absurd

[1] Ibid., p. 119.   [2] Ibid., p. 137.

to talk of the illegality of their actions or to suppose that they can exceed their authority. Bentham does not say, with Hobbes, that the sovereign's power is morally unlimited, nor yet that, if the sovereign limits his power by convention, that convention is never binding. The Hobbesian and the Austinian notions of sovereignty are equally alien to Bentham, though several of the phrases used by Austin in his famous definition are borrowed from the passage just quoted from the *Fragment on Government*. Bentham would not, for instance, deny that a state member of a federal union is a sovereign state.

Bentham assumes that Blackstone never read the third volume of Hume's *Treatise of Human Nature*, from which he says that he himself derived the greatest profit. 'That the foundations of all virtue are laid in utility, is there demonstrated, after a few exceptions made, with the strongest force of evidence: but I see not, any more than Helvetius saw, what need there was for the exceptions.'[1] It may be that there is better evidence that Bentham misunderstood Hume than that Blackstone never read him. For, if Bentham had understood Hume, he would easily have seen what need there was for the exceptions. Hume's evidence for the main rule was, in fact, of precisely the same character as his evidence for the exceptions: namely, the moral behaviour of mankind. Bentham does not quarrel with the facts Hume gives as evidence for the exceptions; he does not even discuss these facts or consider the possibility that they may be evidence against an exclusively utilitarian system of morals. He merely treats Hume's main contention as if it were self-evident, and then blames Hume for supposing that there is evidence which makes it necessary to qualify it. Bentham considers himself as much an empiricist as Hume, but in fact he is often very much the opposite. He treats what he ought to believe are generalizations from experience as if they were self-evident propositions; and he does not trouble to dispose of what might appear to be evidence against them. The truth is that Bentham is not much interested in the logical status of his borrowed principles; and so finds it easy to extract what he wants from Hume, to misunderstand him, and still to be grateful to him. He tells us that, when he read the third volume of Hume's *Treatise*, he felt as if the scales had fallen from his eyes. 'I then, for the first time, learnt to call the cause of the people

[1] Ibid., p. 154 note.

the cause of virtue . . . I learnt to see that utility was the test and measure of all virtue; of loyalty as much as any; and that the obligation to minister to general happiness, was an obligation paramount to and inclusive of every other. Having thus got the instruction I stood in need of, I sat down to take my profit of it.'[1] Bentham thinks he has taken over what is essential to Hume's ethical system, rejecting only what is inconsistent with it. But what he does is to reject the qualifications and subtleties that make the system plausible; and because he misunderstands what he is rejecting, he has no misgivings.

One of the first consequences of Bentham's profiting from the instruction of Hume, is that he 'bids adieu' to the original contract. The theory of the original contract was, he thinks, historically useful, because it provided an excuse, at a time when a better was wanting, to justify popular resistance to bad kings. But how, he asks, are the people to know whether the king has broken his contract? If he promised to promote their happiness, then the test for a breach of contract is utilitarian; and the utilitarian argument for resistance would still remain even if there had been no contract. On the other hand, those who assert that the king promises to obey the law, will yet admit that his every illegal action, however petty, does not justify resistance. But the only test that will enable us to distinguish between trivial and serious illegalities is the test of utility. Besides, the duty to keep promises is itself only intelligible because the keeping of promises is to the advantage of society; so that all the arguments of the contract theorists are reduced to arguments from utility. As soon as this is understood, the notion of the social contract, always unhistorical, ceases to be useful. Bentham gives us his own opinion in these words: 'they (the subjects) should obey so long as the probable mischiefs of obedience are less than the probable mischiefs of resistance . . . (and) *taking the whole body together*, it is their duty to obey, just as long as it is their interest, and no longer'.[2] This is the doctrine of Hume in the words of Bentham.

Blackstone had argued, following Montesquieu, that the British Constitution in the eighteenth century was of the mixed type, having monarchical, aristocratic and democratic features in it; and also that it was an example of the separation of powers.

---

[1] Ibid., p. 154 note.   [2] Ibid., p. 160.

Bentham, in the *Fragment on Government*, differs from Blackstone on both these matters. Many of Bentham's arguments against the view that Britain has a mixed constitution are pedantic. For instance, he argues that Blackstone has distinguished the three main types of government (monarchy, aristocracy, and democracy) by determining where the legislative power resides. But the King of England, says Bentham, when he acts as a monarch (i.e. on his own authority and through subordinates) has only executive power, while he no longer, in practice, makes use of his legislative veto. Such an argument, advanced in George III's reign, clearly takes no account of political realities. A much better point against Blackstone, that the House of Commons under George III was not democratic, does not occur to Bentham. He does, however, show that Blackstone's argument, that the British Constitution is the best because it combines all the virtues of the three main types, could be used just as easily to prove that it is the worst, because it combines all their vices.

Bentham is more happily inspired in his attack on Blackstone's notion that the separation of powers was exhibited in the British political system of his day, under which the king could create peers, get placemen into the House of Commons, and dissolve Parliament.

The limitations of Bentham as a moral philosopher are nowhere better illustrated than in the fifth chapter of the *Fragment on Government*. He has already told us, earlier in the book, that the 'obligation to minister to general happiness, (is) an obligation paramount to and inclusive of every other'. But now, only eighty pages later, he says: 'That is my duty to do, which I am liable to be punished, according to law, if I do not do: this is the original, ordinary and proper sense of the word duty'.[1] And in the note on the same page, he says: 'One may conceive three sorts of duties, political, moral and religious; correspondent to the three sorts of sanctions by which they are enforced: . . .'[2] Bentham then describes the sanctions, which are punishment in the ordinary sense of the word, punishment expected at the hands of the Supreme Being, and 'various mortifications resulting from the ill-will of persons uncertain and variable—the community in general . . .'[3] If any one should persist, Bentham continues in a note on another page, 'in asserting it to be a

[1] Ibid., p. 234.   [2] Ibid., p. 234 note.   [3] Ibid., p. 234 note.

duty, but without meaning it should be understood that it is on any one of these three accounts that he looks upon it as such; all he then asserts is his own internal sentiment: all he means then is, that he feels himself pleased or displeased at the thought of the point of conduct in question, but without being able to tell why. In this case he should e'en say so: and not seek to give an undue influence to his own suffrage, by delivering it in terms that purport to declare the voice either of God, or of the law, or of the people'.[1] Nothing could better illustrate than this passage to how little purpose Bentham had studied Hume's ethical system, which rests entirely on the internal sentiments on which Bentham here pours scorn. Bentham's definition of duty is similar to those offered by Hobbes and by Paley; and would appear to belong more properly to psychological hedonism than to utilitarianism. But Bentham, unlike Hobbes and Paley, never understood precisely what view it was to which he was committing himself. Having thus defined duty, he goes on to discuss the question whether the supreme governors of the state have duties. His conclusion is that they cannot have political (by which he means legal) but may have religious and moral duties, for they are liable to the punishment of God and may also become the objects of popular ill-will. To have a duty, to be under an obligation, is, therefore, for Bentham, the same thing as to be impelled to action or inaction from fear of the evil that some other rational being would do to the agent if he failed to do what was required of him. Yet, in the same note in which he tells us this, Bentham also suggests quite another explanation. He says that he would be glad to see the supreme governors make laws 'because I am persuaded that it is for the benefit of the community that they . . . should do so. This is enough to warrant me in my opinion for saying that they ought to do it'.[2] Taken literally, these few lines make nonsense, for they assert that it is because Bentham believes that governmental legislation would benefit the community that he is right in asserting that the governors ought to make laws. Exercising towards Bentham a charity he rarely extended to Blackstone, we may interpret him as meaning that, if he is right in thinking that governmental legislation would benefit the community, then he is right in holding that the government ought to make laws. But, in that case, duty is no longer what Bentham says

[1] Ibid., p. 235 note.   [2] Ibid., p. 235 note.

it is, for it is now implied that duty is the obligation to promote the public good; and the notion of sanctions is left out of the account altogether.

Having defined the word 'duty' to his own satisfaction, without a trace of awareness that he has stumbled on difficulties that need to be explained before his definition can be accepted, Bentham takes leave of his reader, apologizing for the tedious war of words with which he has wearied him. Had there been sense in Blackstone, he would have attached himself to it. Some of his readers may object that to attack nonsense is to waste time, but his real purpose has been to teach the student 'to place more confidence in his own strength, and less in the infallibility of great names: to help him to emancipate his judgment from the shackles of authority; . . . to warn him not to pay himself with words . . .'[1] Bentham was an amiable but not a modest man. He never knew how well he had performed his task, for he had not only deliberately exposed the intellectual failings of Blackstone but had also involuntarily exhibited his own.

3. *The Introduction to the Principles of Morals and Legislation*

This book was published thirteen years after the appearance of the *Fragment on Government*, and it is the most important of all Bentham's writings. It opens with an often-quoted passage containing so many ambiguities that it will not be possible to deal with them all. 'Nature', says Bentham, 'has placed mankind under the governance of two sovereign masters, pain and pleasure. It is for them alone to point out what we ought to do, as well as to determine what we shall do . . . They govern us in all we do . . . In words a man may pretend to abjure their empire: but in reality he will remain subject to it all the while. The principle of utility recognises this subjection, . . .' And then, in a note at the bottom of the first page, Bentham tells us what the principle of utility is. It is 'that principle which states the greatest happiness of all those whose interest is in question, as being the right and proper, and only right and proper and universally desirable, end of human action: . .' In another note on the next page, Bentham says that the principle

[1] Ibid., p. 240.

of utility 'may be taken for an act of the mind; a sentiment . . . which, when applied to an action, approves of its utility, as that quality of it by which the measure of approbation or disapprobation bestowed upon it ought to be governed'.

These passages from the first two pages of a book whose one purpose is to make clear the fundamental principles on which the author rests his system, betray the little thought that was devoted to their composition. Bentham was not primarily a philosopher. He was anxious to have done with first principles as quickly as possible and to settle down to more congenial tasks. But the attentive reader cannot help but ask many questions. What does Bentham mean by the sovereign mastery of pleasure and pain? Does he mean that men necessarily seek their own pleasure and avoid their own pain? Or does he mean that to promote pleasure and to avoid pain, whosever they may be, is always their motive? In other words, is he or is he not committed to the egoistic hedonism expounded by Hobbes? What does he mean when he says that pleasure and pain determine what men ought to do as well as what they will do? May we infer from this that all men always do their duty? What was in Bentham's mind when he said that the principle of utility recognizes this subjection? If men always seek their own pleasure and avoid their own pain, how can the greatest happiness of *all* those whose interest is in question be the only right and proper end of human action? What is meant by calling this end universally desirable? On the other hand, if what men always seek is not only their own pleasure but other people's as well, what is the point of saying that it is their duty to do what they will do in any case? There is, no doubt, nothing self-contradictory in the assertion that it is a man's duty to do what he will do in any case. A benevolent and omniscient God would always do his duty and could not do otherwise. Does Bentham mean us to understand that men, though they always seek the greatest happiness of those whose interest is in question, do not always know where to find it, and that it therefore behoves Bentham to show them how they may do so? But it is clear, from what Bentham says elsewhere, that he does not believe that men are always benevolent. On the contrary, he is more often inclined to think them always, or nearly always, selfish. Again, what does Bentham mean by saying that the principle of utility 'may be taken for an act of the mind; a sentiment . . . which, when applied to an action, approves of its utility'? This act of mind or sentiment is said to be approval of utility, and in the same sentence utility is defined 'as that quality of it (an action) by which the measure of approbation or disapprobation bestowed upon it ought to be governed'.[1] Can we understand Bentham to mean that the principle of utility is itself a sentiment: the approval of a habit whereby men approve of actions that cause happiness and disapprove of those that cause unhappiness? That this is not the right interpretation is suggested by what Bentham says about fourteen pages later: 'What one expects to find in a principle is something that points out some external consideration, as a means of warranting and guiding the internal sentiments of approbation or disapprobation.'[2]

All the questions I have put (and most of which I shall not answer because Bentham's words suggest no answer) are perfectly fair questions. By this I mean that they are not questions designed merely to call attention to Bentham's careless manner of speaking, while, with a little good will, the reader can easily get at his meaning. The truth is that it is not possible to make sense of what Bentham is saying. Nothing can be done except to indicate the more important ambiguities with which these short quotations abound. It seems to me that Bentham, without quite knowing what he is doing, is trying to reconcile two couples of irreconcilable doctrines: egoistic hedonism with utilitarianism, on the one hand; and a psychological with an objective theory of morals on the other.

When Bentham tries to tell us what his moral theory is, he succeeds in telling us very little. But when he begins to apply the principles he has failed to define, it is, I think, possible to get some idea of what they are. Though he often makes statements incompatible with them, I think it is fair to say that Bentham usually adheres to the following principles: (i) that nothing is in itself desirable except pleasure and the relief of pain; (ii) that one man's pleasure is in itself as desirable as any other man's; (iii) that the right action is always the one which the prospective agent believes to be, under the circumstances, productive of the greatest happiness;

---

[1] *Introduction* to *Principles of Morals and Legislation*, p. 2 note. (Oxford 1876 edition.)

[2] *Ibid.*, p. 16.

(iv) that man is predominantly selfish but is capable of benevolence;
(v) that laws and punishments ought, in every political society,
to be so adjusted that, with the least possible restraint of liberty
and infliction of pain, they ensure that men will, from selfish
motives, act in ways that will promote other men's happiness as
well as their own.

The first six chapters of the *Introduction to the Principles of Morals
and Legislation* are, perhaps, the worst in the book. Quite apart
from the ambiguities in the first few pages, to which I have already
alluded, there are many others; and there are fallacies as well.
The first two chapters merely make more elaborate the confusion
already created in the first two pages. The third chapter, which
classifies the sources of pain and pleasure, is clear enough; but the
fourth, which gives us the rules for estimating the value (i.e.
measuring the quantity) of pains and pleasures, turns its back on life
and parodies reason. Bentham tells us that the value of a lot of
pleasure or pain varies with its intensity, its duration, its certainty
or uncertainty, its propinquity or remoteness, its fecundity ('or the
chance it has of being followed by sensations of the same kind'), its
purity ('or the chance it has of not being followed by sensations of
the opposite kind') and its extent (or the number of persons who
experience it). These are what Bentham calls the seven 'dimensions'
of pleasure and pain; and he believes that by operating with them we
can assess the value, by which he means the quantity, of any sum of
pleasure or pain. He admits that in practice such calculations can
seldom be made with accuracy, but he supposes that they are in
principle possible. He says: 'It is not to be expected that this process
should be strictly pursued previously to every moral judgment, or
to every legislative and judicial operation. It may, however, be
always kept in view; and as near as the process actually pursued on
these occasions approaches to it, so near will such a process approach
to the character of an exact one'.[1] In other words, it is only
because it is impracticable to do so that we do not make such
accurate calculations; but we do in fact make rough ones, and, no
doubt, if we had the time and all the facts at our disposal we could
make completely accurate calculations. This is what Bentham
believes; whereas the truth is that even an omniscient God could not
make such calculations, for the very notion of them is impossible.

[1] Ibid., p. 31.

F

The intensity of a pleasure cannot be measured against its duration, nor its duration against its certainty or uncertainty, nor this latter property against its propinquity or remoteness. Of all the 'dimensions' mentioned by Bentham, only two couples are commensurable, duration with extent and fecundity with purity. We can say that a pleasure or pain of a given intensity experienced by a person for two minutes is equal to that same pleasure or pain experienced by two persons for one minute; and we can also say of a pleasure that its fecundity exceeds its purity, if, for instance, there is one chance in four of its being followed by another pleasure and only one chance in five of its not being followed by a pain.

There is no need to labour an obvious and simple point. Bentham ought not to have talked of the 'dimensions' of pleasure and pain; he ought to have realized that when we are said to 'multiply three dimensions' to discover a volume, the three dimensions are all of them linear, and that the numbers, which are all that we in fact multiply, represent units of equal length. He saw an analogy where there was none. *He also confused measurements of quantity with comparisons of effects.* When a man has to choose between two alternative pleasures, one of which is mild but lasting and the other intense but brief, he never can choose the greater, for the simple reason that neither is the greater. What he can do, however, is to choose the one he desires the more intensely. Now it may well be that there are certain psychological laws which, if we knew them, would enable us to say that the intensity of men's desires for pleasures vary in such and such ways with the intensity of the pleasures desired and in such and such other ways with their estimated duration, their certainty and uncertainty, their propinquity and remoteness, their fecundity, their purity and their extent. If there are such laws, then, if we could know them, we could also calculate that a certain lot of pleasure (to use Bentham's phrase) is likely to be more intensely desired by most men than a certain other lot. But this calculation would be of a kind quite different from the one described by Bentham.

It has sometimes been argued in favour of Bentham's felicific calculus that, whatever the theoretical objections against it, men often do estimate the consequences of alternative possible actions and then choose to perform the one which is likely, in their opinion, to produce the greatest happiness. Bentham himself says of his theory: 'Nor is this a novel and unwarranted, any more than it is a useless theory. In all this there is nothing but what the practice of mankind, wheresoever they have a clear view of their own interest, is perfectly conformable to.'[1] It is, of course, quite true that men do compare the consequences of alternative actions, but this does not mean that they calculate quantities of pleasure. What they do is to get what information they can about the alternatives and then make up their minds in favour of one of them. They analyse each of the alternatives, taking into account as many of its constituents as they have the leisure to do, but this taking into account is not itself, except on rare occasions, a calculation of quantities, however rough and ready; it is merely the process of becoming more intimately acquainted with each alternative separately. We choose between alternative consequences largely as we choose between paintings or other objects of art. In both cases, we consider the alternative wholes and their constituent details as carefully as time and temperament permit, but we do not add, subtract, divide or multiply. Or rather, whereas no calculation at all is possible in the latter case, it is so, to some extent, in the former; for we can make quantitative measurements of duration, extent and chance.

We cannot, however, infer from this that the legislator need make little use of the information supplied to him by the statistician. Experience can, in such cases, furnish us with two sets of relevant generalizations; it can, for instance, teach us that most men prefer some pleasures to others, that some pleasures pall more quickly than others, that men of different ages and different social classes have different preferences, that they will prefer a mild and durable pleasure to an intense and brief one under certain circumstances but not others; and experience can also teach us what are the social and economic conditions that will enable most men to have as many opportunities as possible to enjoy the pleasures they prefer. In other words, it is theoretically possible to give men as much of what they want as they have time to enjoy (or, rather, on the utilitarian hypothesis, as much of what is good for them, in the sense of as much as they would want and have time to enjoy, if they were aware of all the relevant considerations). And the relevant considerations are largely those very things which Bentham unwisely called the dimensions of pleasure—duration, intensity, certainty and

[1] Ibid., p. 32.

uncertainty, propinquity, fecundity and so on. Men, in establishing their preferences, take these considerations into account (as far as they are in practice able to do so); but the process does not, except to a very limited extent, involve a calculation of quantities of pleasure and pain. Once these preferences are established, they can be studied, their frequencies can be calculated, and together with other statistical information, vital, social and economic, they can serve as a guide to policy. Calculations of this kind are likely to give the most imperfect results; the margin of error is almost certain to be great. But, though their utility must be often doubtful, they are, in principle, possible. An omniscient being could carry them out with perfect accuracy, and if he were also omnipotent and benevolent, would no doubt act accordingly. He could then quite properly be said to be promoting the greatest happiness of the greatest number, provided it were understood that *no measurable quantity of pleasure was in question*. Moreover, if such a being could realize such a policy, there is no reason why a human government should not try to do so. Utilitarianism does not stand or fall with Bentham's felicific calculus. Such a calculus is impossible, not merely in practice but also in theory. But the utilitarian can have recourse to other calculations, which are, in fact, possible, though they must always, human nature and human knowledge being what they are, be most imperfect. That, however, is not in itself a serious objection to a theory of morals.

His first six chapters completed, Bentham leaves behind him the analysis of his fundamental principles; and we may gratefully follow him out of the quagmire on to firmer ground. 'The business of government,' Bentham tells us, 'is to promote the happiness of society, by punishing and rewarding.'[1] Now, Bentham's task, in the rest of the book, is to establish the rules that a government ought to follow if it is to promote as much of this happiness as it can at the cost of the least possible amount of punishment. Every now and again, Bentham uses the language of the felicific calculus, talking of quantities of pleasure and pain and not merely of the number of persons who experience, and the times during which they experience, these pleasures and pains. Nor does he take into account the orders and frequencies of men's preferences. He often talks, in fact, as if he were advising legislators and judges how to make

[1] Ibid., p. 70.

calculations which it is plainly impossible to make. But all the misleading language can be ignored, and Bentham's rules can be treated as if they were rules for making possible calculations. Once this is done, it is easy to see how much that is really valuable his book contains. What Bentham teaches us, often with great vigour and ingenuity, is how to prevent as many offences as possible as efficiently as we can and at the cost of no greater suffering than is required for the purpose.

Bentham begins by analysing the offence for which the culprit is to be punished. His analysis is extremely complicated, but it is necessary to master only a small part of it in order to understand the general character of his theory of punishment. The distinction to which Bentham attaches the greatest importance is that between a man's motive and his intention when he acts. By an intention he means those consequences of a man's action that he expected would follow upon it. By a motive he means the desire for pleasure or for relief from pain that prompted the action. Bentham's definitions are not as simple as the ones I have offered, and there is more than a little about them that is ambiguous. He defines a motive as 'the internal perception of any individual lot of pleasure or pain, the expectation of which is looked upon as calculated to determine you to act in such and such a manner'.[1] He thinks that by using such language he can give greater precision to his ideas. The result is that his readers often cannot guess what he means by the long sentences in which he defines his terms, and can get his meaning only by considering how he uses them. Those definitions of motive and intention which make sense of the general drift of Bentham's argument must be taken to be correct, even if they do not much resemble the ones he offers. We may therefore take it that the motive is the desire for whose satisfaction the act is done, and the intention the expected consequences of it. The expectation, of course, is the agent's, and the actual consequences may be quite different from those expected. The tendency to act from a certain kind of motive Bentham calls a disposition. He makes many other distinctions, not all of them defensible, but these are the only ones of which we need take notice.

These distinctions made, Bentham goes on to say that no motive is in itself either good or bad, for any motive may sometimes lead

[1] Ibid., p. 99.

to actions having bad consequences and at other times to actions having good ones. Lust, cruelty and avarice, he tells us, are called bad motives, but they are in themselves the same motives as sexual desire, desire to inflict pain, and reluctance to part with what one possesses. These motives can lead to good consequences as well as to bad ones; and it is only when they lead to bad ones that they are called lust, cruelty and avarice. Motives give birth to intentions and intentions can be either good or bad. The moralist and the legislator are primarily interested in men's intentions, in the goodness and the badness of the consequences that they intend should follow upon their actions. Men's motives concern the moralist and the legislator only indirectly. For although all motives are in themselves morally neutral, some more often than others give birth to good intentions or else to bad ones.

Many people, including Leslie Stephen, have criticized Bentham for saying that the motives from which men act are morally indifferent. It may be, in practice, a rule that serves the legislator and the judge well enough, for they can hardly be expected to discover men's motives. All that matters to them is that men should do some actions and forbear from others; and their only business must therefore be to apply rewards and punishments in such a way that this end is attained. But the morality of the action cannot, these critics say, be independent of the motive from which it is done. Their difference from Bentham may be smaller than they think. What Bentham means when he says that motives are morally neutral is that any kind of desire may be the cause of either good or bad intentions. A man may desire to eat, and to satisfy his hunger he may either get food from his own larder or he may steal it from his neighbour's. The desire in either case is the same, but the two actions prompted by it are quite different. So too, if a man wishes to give pain to another, his desire may lead to a good intention. He may, for instance, intend to punish a criminal. It is only when he desires to inflict pain on some one who does not deserve it that we condemn him. When Bentham says that a motive is morally neutral, he is thinking of a naked desire without taking into account the circumstances in which it arose or the intention to which it gives birth. But when we say that the morality of the action depends above all upon the motive, we always take into account the circumstances. Otherwise, we could hardly distinguish between ingrati-

tude and indifference, malice and the desire to inflict pain, praise
and flattery, benevolence and indulgence. Bentham's doctrine has
an air of paradox but it is not nearly as offensive as it sounds. And
no one could be more anxious than he to maintain that men rightly
disapprove of malice, jealousy, envy and all the other vices.

Bentham distinguishes between the various kinds of motives
according to the relative frequencies with which they give birth
to good and bad intentions. Benevolence, or good will, has the
greatest tendency to coincide with utility. It is the only purely
social (by which Bentham means altruistic) motive. Next in order
of preference come love of reputation, desire for friendship, and
religion. Bentham calls them semi-social motives, because they are
partly self-regarding and partly altruistic. Of the purely self-regarding motives, such as physical desire, love of power, self-preservation,
Bentham says only that they are less likely than the social and semi-
social motives to give birth to good intentions, but he does not
establish an order of preference among them. He probably thought
that the self-regarding motives do not, except malevolence, have a
marked tendency to produce bad rather than good intentions or
vice versa. The motives that often give birth to bad intentions
he calls 'seducing' or 'corrupting', and those that restrain men from
giving way to this seduction he calls 'tutelary'. Benevolence and the
semi-social motives are usually tutelary. Milder than malevolence,
they are also more constant.

After an elaborate analysis of actions, consequences, motives
and intentions, of which I have given only the barest outline,
Bentham goes on to establish the rules which ought to guide the
legislator in deciding what punishments are to be given to offenders.
He begins by asserting that 'all punishment is mischief: all punishment in itself is evil. Upon the principle of utility . . . it ought
only to be admitted in as far as it promises to exclude some greater
evils'.[1] It therefore immediately follows that punishment ought not
to be inflicted where it is groundless (i.e. where there is no mischief
for it to prevent); where it is inefficacious; where it is too expensive
(i.e. where the mischief it would produce exceeds the mischief it
would prevent); where it is needless (i.e. where the mischief could
be prevented in some other less painful manner).

Punishment seeks to control men's future actions. If we are to

[1] Ibid., p. 170.

interpret Bentham's meaning strictly, then no one can deserve punishment; it can merely be right that he should be punished. Punishment can seek to control the offender's future actions, in which case it is either reformatory or disabling; or else it can seek to control other people's future actions, in which case it is deterrent. It usually seeks to do both. If it gives satisfaction to the injured party, so much the better; but this is not an important part of its purpose.

Bentham gives us nine rules for the infliction of punishments. They are mostly mere rules of common sense, and there is no need to comment on them. Bentham himself thought otherwise, but it is easy to see that, though they involve calculation, they do not involve the felicific calculus dreamt of by him. These rules are: (i) The punishment must be great enough to outweigh the profit of the offence to the offender; (ii) the greater the mischief of the offence, the greater the punishment; (iii) and (iv) are mere corollaries of (ii); (v) punishment should never be greater than the least amount required to make it effective; (vi) the sensibility of the offender must always be taken into account; (vii) the more uncertain it is that the offender will suffer it, the greater the punishment should be; (viii) the more distant it is, the greater it should be; and (ix) if the offence is of a kind likely to be habitual with the offender, the punishment must be increased to outweigh the profit not only of the immediate offence but of the other offences probably committed with impunity. If these simple rules now appear obvious to us, we must not, for that reason, belittle Bentham's service to mankind in enunciating them. At the time that he wrote, they had for centuries been ignored by the legislators and judges of Europe.

Bentham, anticipating possible criticism of his rules, says: 'There are some, perhaps, who . . . may look upon the nicety employed in the adjustment of such rules as so much labour lost: for gross ignorance, they will say, never troubles itself about laws, and passion does not calculate. But the evil of ignorance admits of cure: and . . . when matters of such importance as pain and pleasure are at stake, and these in the highest degree . . . who is there that does not calculate? Men calculate, some with less exactness, indeed, and some with more: but all men calculate.'[1] Bentham is quite

[1] Ibid., p. 187.

right. All men calculate, for if they did not it would be impossible, not only for others to govern them, but for themselves to live. But the calculations they make, necessary and crude though they are, are not described by Bentham, either in this or in any other of his works.

Much the longest chapter of the *Introduction to the Principles of Morals and Legislation* is devoted to a classification of offences. In it Bentham repeats the arguments, already advanced in the *Fragment on Government*, in favour of what he calls both a natural and a scientific system of classification, which groups offences according to the influence they have upon the happiness of mankind. 'What a state', he asks, 'would botany, for example, be in if the classes were so contrived that no common characters could be found for them?'[1] But that, he thought, was precisely the case with jurisprudence at the time that he was writing. It was for him to create rational order where there was none, to do for jurisprudence what Linnaeus had done for botany. Bentham's classification of offences covers a hundred pages, but as the details of its elaboration involve no important moral or political principles, it is not necessary to consider it.

So much, then, for the second of the two works of Bentham of which posterity still takes the most notice. In these two works he put forward most of the maxims and definitions that he considered fundamental to his whole system; and it is with them that his reputation as a moral and political theorist stands or falls. It is clear that, in both these capacities, Bentham was greatly the inferior of Hume, from whom he borrowed so much, and often without understanding what it was that he borrowed. Two incompatible couples, utilitarianism and egoistic hedonism, a psychological and an *a priori* system of morals, lay quietly side by side in his capacious mind, and their host had not a suspicion that the guests he was entertaining were so strangely assorted. Leslie Stephen was not wrong when, in his book on the English Utilitarians, he said that Bentham knew little of psychology and ethics. Yet Stephen's final verdict was rightly a generous one. 'However imperfect his system might be, considered as a science of society and human nature . . . (his) method involved a thorough-going examination of the whole body of laws, and a resolution to apply a searching test to every law. If that test was not so unequivocal or ultimate as he

[1] Ibid., p. 300 note.

fancied, it yet implied the constant application of such considerations as must always carry weight, and, perhaps, be always the dominant considerations, with the actual legislator or jurist.'[1] Stephen's conclusion was that Bentham's test, though not all-sufficient, is good enough for the purposes to which Bentham put it. I would agree with this verdict, with one most important qualification. The test that is good enough for Bentham's purposes is not the test described by Bentham; it may fairly be said to involve the notion of the greatest happiness of the greatest number only if that greatest happiness is defined quite otherwise than Bentham defined it.

4. His Radicalism

After the failure of his *Panopticon* scheme and his meeting James Mill in 1808, Bentham became as thorough-going a radical as Paine had ever been. But to justify his radicalism he used quite different arguments. He had always believed that every man always desires his own greatest happiness; and also that the only proper end of government is to promote the greatest happiness of the greatest number. On the other hand, he had now learnt, especially since the rejection of his favourite project, that the actual end of every government is the greatest happiness of the governors. He soon concluded that the fundamental problem of government is to make these two ends coincide; to make it the selfish interest of the governors to promote the greatest happiness of the greatest number. The device that can ensure the coincidence of these two ends is democracy. Bentham, however, recognized that the direct participation of the people in government is not practicable in large countries; he therefore advocated every sort of device that would increase the dependence of their representatives on the people. He favoured annual parliaments, the abolition of the monarchy and the House of Lords, the secret ballot, female suffrage, the election of the Prime Minister by Parliament, the appointment of civil servants by competitive examination. All government, for Bentham as for Paine, is a necessary evil; and it follows that every government must be anxiously watched by the citizens lest it should acquire more power than it needs to carry out its limited duties.

The idea that government is an evil, but that it is, unfortunately,

[1] Leslie Stephen, *The English Utilitarians*, Vol. I, p. 271.

a necessary evil, is a very old one. It is suggested by the early Christian belief that coercive government, like slavery and private property, is the consequence of man's fall, of his sinfulness. It stands at the very centre of Hobbes's system, for what is the purpose of Leviathan except to create the fear that casts out fear? Neither Paine nor the French revolutionaries[1] were good Christians, but they shared with the Christian Fathers the belief that liberty is intrinsically good and that man has a natural right to it. If liberty is good, then government must, they thought, be evil; and its only justification can be that, by restraining man's passions, it removes more obstacles to liberty than it creates. The utilitarians arrive at the same conclusion from a different premise. Their argument is taken from Hobbes. Government is evil, not because liberty is good but because pain is evil; its only justification is that its coercive action creates less pain than it prevents.

Bentham was an egalitarian in the same sense as he was a radical and a liberal. Equality is not desirable for its own sake; all that is so desirable is the greatest happiness of the greatest number. This is the one fundamental principle; the limits of liberty and equality are determined by it and by the lessons of experience. That all men should be treated as if they were equal means, for Bentham, no more than this: that no differences between them that are irrelevant to the legislator's fundamental purpose, the promotion of the greatest happiness of the greatest number, ought to be taken into account. Paley was an egalitarian in exactly this same sense. Paley's God, no doubt, would treat all men as equals, and yet allow the greatest inequalities between them. If Paley approved these inequalities and Bentham did not, it was not because their principles were different but only because they differed about a matter of fact. Paley believed that nearly all such inequalities are a means to the greatest happiness of the greatest number, whereas Bentham, especially after he had met James Mill, came to believe that many of them are not.

It may be instructive, before we part company with Bentham, to notice how closely his arguments for radicalism resemble those of

[1] The Jacobins, when they controlled it, were very willing that the state should be strong, however great the sacrifice of individual liberty. But then, the Jacobins were unlike most French revolutionaries. They were a ruthless minority who acquired power largely because they did not share the liberal prejudices of most Frenchmen active in politics.

Hobbes in favour of the absolute power of governments. Every man, says Hobbes, is completely selfish, but painful experience teaches him that he has one great interest in common with all other men: the existence of an absolute sovereign with power to coerce them all. Every man, says Bentham, is almost completely selfish, but painful experience teaches him that he has one great interest in common with all other men: the existence of a government that seeks to promote the greatest happiness of the greatest number and can be trusted to do so only if it is responsible to all the people and jealously watched by them. This argument of Bentham's is hardly consistent with his frequent assertions that the greatest happiness of the greatest number is an ultimate end, for what nobody desires except as a means can hardly be an ultimate end. But we are not to expect from Bentham the degree of consistency that we get from Hobbes.

CHAPTER V

THE RADICAL UTILITARIANS

BENTHAM was not the first utilitarian to turn radical, and before we pass on to James Mill and his friends, we must pause to consider the earliest forms of utilitarian radicalism. Priestley, in his *Essay on the First Principles of Government* (1768), had taken up once again what Hume had considered the fundamental problem of politics, the identification of the interests of the governors with those of the governed. Unlike Hume, Priestley believed that no such identity yet existed in England, and that a considerable measure of reform was needed to establish it. Priestley was a very moderate democrat, but the arguments he used in favour of reform are certainly utilitarian in character.

Burke's *Reflections on the French Revolution* moved two men to make a reply to him. The first was James Mackintosh, who, in his *Vindiciae Gallicae*, criticized Burke for his praise of mixed government, of the division of powers and complex political institutions reflecting the complex structure of society. These ideas Burke had got from Montesquieu, one of whose favourite theses it was that simple laws and simple institutions best suit the despotic state. Most of his arguments against Burke, Mackintosh borrowed from Bentham, but whereas Bentham felt only curiosity towards the activities of the French revolutionaries, Mackintosh, until he was thrown off his course by the Jacobin Terror, espoused their cause. He tried to reconcile his utilitarian principles with a defence of the doctrine of the Rights of Man. Mackintosh admitted that the question of the origins of government has no philosophical importance, that what really matters is the end that it promotes, and that this end is happiness. But he held that the language of the Rights of Man still has its use, if it is understood to be a sort of shorthand that needs to be translated at length. 'When I assert,' he says, 'that a man has a right to life, liberty, etc., I only mean to enunciate a moral maxim founded on a general interest, which prohibits any attack on these possessions.' The proper retort to Mackintosh is that this is a mistranslation, for it is certainly not what the American and French revolutionaries meant when they used the language of the Rights of Man.

1. PAINE

Far more important than Priestley and Mackintosh was Tom Paine, the greatest English radical of his day. Like Burke, Paine was not a member of the family but was a sort of second cousin to the utilitarians. The arguments that Paine uses in his most famous book are just the kind that seemed excellent to the French revolutionaries, who had many of them read Rousseau but not Helvetius or Hume. Paine's fundamental thesis in the *Rights of Man* is that every man, merely because he is a sentient and a rational being, possesses certain inalienable rights. Some of these, such as the freedom of thought, he can exercise without more ado in the privacy of his own mind; but the others must be secured to him against the encroachments of his fellow-men. He needs a guarantee, and this he can find only in the existence of a government strong enough to force his neighbours to respect his rights. Now, the only way to ensure that the government will do just this and not attempt to do more is to make it democratic and to define its powers in a written constitution.

But in his book *Common Sense* (1776), and also in the second part of his *Rights of Man*, which appeared in 1792, only a few months after the first part, Paine used arguments that are much more utilitarian in character. On the first page of *Common Sense*, he says: 'Some writers have so confounded society with government, as to leave little or no distinction between them: whereas they are not only different but have different origins. Society is produced by our wants, and government by our wickedness; the former promotes our happiness positively, by uniting our affections: the latter negatively, by restraining our vices. The one encourages intercourse, the other creates distinctions. The first is a patron, the last a punisher'.

'Society in every state is a blessing, but government, even in its best state, is but a necessary evil . . . Government, like dress, is the badge of lost innocence. . . . For were the impulses of conscience clear, uniform, and irresistibly obeyed, man would need no other lawgiver; but that not being the case, he finds it necessary to surrender up a part of his property to furnish means for the protection of the rest; and this he is induced to do by the same prudence which in every other case advises him, out of two evils, to chuse the least. Wherefore, security being the true design and end of government, it unanswerably follows, that whatever form thereof appears most likely to ensure it to us with the least expense, and greatest benefit, is preferable to all others.'

It was the opinion of Plato that the first society was the product of men's wants, or rather of their need to co-operate for the satisfaction of these wants, and that this first society was prior to government. This same idea was present in Hume's mind when, in the third Book of his *Treatise*, he rejected the theory that 'men are utterly incapable of society without government'. It is also to be found in Rousseau's *Discourse on the Origins of Inequality among Men*. It is an old idea; as is also the one, to which neither Plato nor Hume would have subscribed, that government is a necessary evil. What is more interesting, however, is that Paine, on this first page of *Common Sense*, when he is setting out his fundamental principles, makes no mention of natural rights. His argument is, at bottom, the same as Bentham's. The end is the happiness of mankind, who will, especially in the economic sphere, be drawn by their own interests into co-operation. But they cannot be relied upon always to co-operate peacefully. Hence the necessity of government, always in itself an evil, because its function is essentially negative and punitive. Paine then goes on to argue that the form of government most likely to carry out this function efficiently and cheaply is democracy. We have, therefore, in the first few pages of *Common Sense* the gist of the utilitarian argument for democracy at least thirty years before Bentham became a radical.

In the second part of *Rights of Man*, Paine resumes and develops the argument he first advanced in *Common Sense*, but this time with a difference. In 1776, Paine had suggested that, men's wants being greater than their power to satisfy them, their own interest had led them first to co-operate in society and later to institute government to preserve the advantages gained in society. But in the second part of *Rights of Man*, he goes further. Nature, he says, 'has not only forced [men] into society, by a diversity of wants, which the reciprocal aid of each other can supply, but she has implanted in [man] a system of social affections, which, though not necessary to its [society's] existence, are essential to his happiness. There is no period in life when this love for society ceases to act. It begins and ends with our being'.[1] It thus appears that, while self-interest alone is strong enough to create and maintain society, a society entirely so maintained would do no more than enable us to satisfy the diversity of our wants. It is through our social affections that we can obtain from society a greater happiness than the mere satisfaction of our physical desires could give us. 'Man,' says Paine, 'is so naturally a creature of society, that it is impossible to put him out of it.'[2] On the other hand, the more perfect the society, the smaller the need for government.

This insistence on the social nature of man is not to be found in Bentham, though he did not deny that there could be society without government. Bentham believed that, whatever the benevolence of men in their dealings with some few of their relatives and friends, they are completely, or almost completely, selfish on all other occasions. If men contrive to live peacefully together in vast societies, this is principally due to two causes: to their knowledge that the means to their happiness is also usually the means to other people's; and to the existence of governments that can restrain them from seeking their own happiness at the expense of other people's. The utility of society and government consists in this: that in the former, men, by co-operation, can reconcile their diverse interests; while the latter possesses a coercive power enabling it to effect this reconciliation whenever it is not the natural product of voluntary co-operation. Paine's social affections, on the other hand, unlike Bentham's benevolence, are not among the mildest of man's sentiments, nor is their usual operation confined to the narrow circle of his relatives and friends. The social affections are with us all our lives, and they are both strong and constant.

2. GODWIN

Paine was not, as we have seen, a consistent utilitarian; indeed, the most widely read part of his most famous book, *Rights of Man*, is incompatible with utilitarianism. But Paine had a great influence on another man, who was a consistent utilitarian and also a more extreme radical than himself. William Godwin's *Political Justice*

[1] Ch. i, para. 3.　　　　　[2] Ch. i, para. 7.

was first published in 1793. At that time, Godwin was already thirty-seven years old. *Political Justice* is therefore not a young man's book, and yet it contains more of the assurance and idealism of youth than any other book written by a utilitarian.

Political Justice, when it was first published, made a great stir among intellectuals. But the reaction, which was the inevitable consequence of England's being at war with Revolutionary France, soon destroyed its popularity. Godwin's reputation was, indeed, among the very first victims of the reaction, for he had advocated both anarchy and communism. It was soon the fashion to set Godwin down for a visionary and to assume that the simplest arguments were sufficient to destroy his system.

There is, nevertheless, much to be said for Godwin's *Political Justice*. It is well-written, lucid and full of good arguments. The assumptions that Godwin makes about the nature of man are not further from the truth than those of most other eighteenth-century political and moral writers. His premises are as plausible as theirs and his arguments usually more lucid and often more cogent. It was his misfortune that they led him to the most extreme conclusions just before the reaction that was to kill all sympathy for revolutionary ideas in England, until it came to birth again about twenty-five years later. It was Godwin's destiny to be famous for a year or two, and then to live out the rest of his life almost forgotten. The Privy Council did, however, once think him a dangerous man and considered prosecuting him for seditious libel. He was saved only by the observation of Pitt that a 'three guinea book could never do much harm among those who had not three shillings to spare'. As a matter of fact, four thousand copies of *Political Justice* were sold, and among their purchasers were many working men, who raised subscriptions to cover the cost.

Like most enthusiasts, Godwin got his ideas from only a few sources. He owed most to Jonathan Edwards' *Enquiry into the Freedom of the Will* (1754), Hartley's *Observations on Man* (1749), and d'Holbach's *Système de la Nature* (1770). It was from these three books that Godwin derived his rigid determinism, and his conviction that the notions of 'desert' and 'merit' have no place in a properly constructed political and moral theory. From Helvetius, Godwin adopted the theory that existing social and political institutions have made man what he is; and that man is the creature,

G

not of heredity, but of environment. Man, therefore, is perfectible. By the use of his reason and the discovery of truth he can alter his environment and improve himself, becoming indefinitely better, though perfection itself may always remain out of his reach. But whereas Helvetius looked to better laws and institutions to improve man, Godwin thought that real improvement required the abolition of both laws and governments.

His anarchy and his communism Godwin derived mainly from French sources, especially from Rousseau and from Mably, but also from Ogilvie's *Essay on the Right of Property in Land,* which appeared two or three years before his own *Political Justice*. Rousseau was not an anarchist, but many of his arguments, especially those to be found in his *Discourse on the Origins of Inequality among Men,* are excellent supports of the anarchist case. Godwin was not a disciple of Rousseau, but he was, perhaps, the only utilitarian to be deeply influenced by the Genevan philosopher.

Godwin was a great borrower from Hume, to whom he owed, as did all the other utilitarians, his rejection of the theory of a social contract. It was also to Hume that Godwin owed his conviction that pleasure and the avoidance of pain are the ultimate objects of human endeavour. His utilitarianism, therefore, Godwin gets directly from Hume. Yet his moral theory is quite different from Hume's. He accepts Hume's doctrine that man is the mere recipient of impressions and ideas. But, unlike Hume, he has no desire to introduce the experimental method into morals. He does not reduce morals to a species of social psychology. Nor does he believe that 'Reason is and ought to be the slave of the passions'. On the contrary, he believes that the laws of justice are eternal and immutable, that they are rules of conduct 'originating in the connection of one percipient being with another'.[1] If I have rightly understood Godwin, his fundamental belief is that it follows from the mere fact that percipient beings are in contact with each other, that they ought to conform to certain rules in their behaviour towards one another. Otherwise, it is impossible to understand his meaning when he calls justice eternal. Godwin was not interested in the epistemological implications of his moral theory. He seems to have regarded Hume's account of man's experience as being, in all essentials, satisfactory. He did not understand that, in that case,

[1] *Political Justice*, Bk. II, ch. ii.

there can be no such thing as eternal justice. It is as true of Godwin as it is of Bentham, that he never understood either the theory of knowledge or the moral system of the great Scottish philosopher.

To Paine, Godwin owed one idea only, but one to which both philosophers attribute the greatest importance: that society and government are two different things. Society, they both agree, is necessary and good; and they also agree that all government is evil. But whereas Paine asserts that it is a necessary evil, Godwin doubts its necessity.

Morality, for Godwin, is no more than the system that teaches us to contribute on all occasions, so far as we can, to the well-being and happiness of every intelligent and sensitive existence. That we ought to do so is, apparently, an axiom of reason; it is a proposition whose truth is evident to us as soon as we have understood it. This is not what Godwin says, but it is what is implied by his saying that justice is eternal and that man can find in it a 'principle of deduction in all cases of moral enquiry'. From this premise, that it is always a man's duty to promote the greatest happiness, Godwin arrives at the conclusion that men have no rights but only duties. This conclusion is not quite as paradoxical as it appears. The rights that Godwin denies are merely discretionary powers. He believes that, since, on nearly all occasions when we have the power to choose, we can do more good by choosing one alternative rather than the others, we are never at liberty, except on unimportant occasions, to do what we please. On the other hand, since men have duties to men, it follows that they also have claims against them. When, therefore, Godwin denies the existence of rights, he is thinking not of claims but of discretionary powers.

But it does not follow, according to Godwin, that, because we are hardly ever entitled to do as we please, other men have the duty to constrain us. Men must not be forced to do their duty; they must do it because they themselves understand that it is their duty. Godwin believes that the exercise of private judgment is 'unspeakably beautiful'. While there is any reasonable hope that persuasion will prevail, we must use argument; and we must never use force except to prevent an immediate injury that cannot otherwise be prevented. That man is born with selfish passions unconquerable by reason and which only force or fear can curb, is a belief that Godwin utterly rejects. When men act wrongly, they always believe, he thinks, that they are acting rightly, or else they pass no moral judgment on their actions. They are guilty either of error or of ignorance. But force is not the proper instrument for the correction of error and ignorance.

Nor, when we do use force, can we justify its use on the ground that it is punishment. According to Godwin, there can be, strictly speaking, no such thing as punishment; for, since the will is not free, no man can help doing what he does, and it is absurd to say that he deserves to suffer. This, however, does not mean that men cannot be virtuous and vicious. The virtuous man habitually chooses to do his duty, while the vicious man has another habit; nor do we approve of the former or disapprove of the latter any the less because both virtue and vice have their necessary causes. This argument of Godwin's is not convincing, since desert no more implies the freedom of the will than does virtue.

The idea that no man can deserve to suffer, and that the justification of punishment is to be found only in its utility is common to all the utilitarians. But Godwin differs from the others in denying that punishment can be reformatory. He thinks that punishment degrades both the offender and the judge. 'If he who employs coercion against me,' says Godwin,[1] 'could mould me to his purpose by argument, no doubt he would. He pretends to punish me because his argument is important, but he really punishes me because his argument is weak.' Godwin also differs from the other utilitarians in denying that its deterrent effect can justify punishment, though the argument he uses does not seem to me to be compatible with his utilitarian principles. If he had contented himself with denying that punishment is ever sufficiently deterrent to justify its use, his argument, whether right or wrong, would have been compatible with his utilitarian premises; but the point he makes is that, unless the punishment is justified for some other reason, it cannot be right to inflict it at all, its deterrent effect making no difference. 'The coercion proposed . . .' says Godwin,[2] 'is either right or wrong. If it be right, it should be employed for its own intrinsic recommendations. If it be wrong, what sort of example does it display?' This argument avoids the real point at issue. The advocates of deterrent punishment are quite willing to admit that no man should be made to suffer for no other reason than

[1] Bk. VII, ch. ii.   [2] Bk. VII, ch. v.

that his suffering would serve as an example to others. Before it can be right to punish him, he must at least have committed the offence in question. Their contention is merely that, if he has committed the offence, then the amount of his punishment ought to be partly determined by the extent to which it is likely to deter other people from committing similar offences. Godwin produces not one argument to show that the deterrent effect of a punishment is not likely to be great enough to justify the suffering it occasions.

Indeed, it is clear that utilitarian considerations count for little in Godwin's condemnation of nearly all coercion. He hates coercion so much that he will have none of it, except where it is very obviously necessary to prevent an immediate danger. That is the real and quite irrational motive behind his denial that its deterrent effect can justify punishment. Since punishment ought never, according to Godwin, to be deterrent, it follows that there is no reason at all why it should be made unpleasant. If a man must be prevented from injuring his fellow-men, and if he will not listen to reason, then it is just to imprison him. But his life in prison must be made as pleasant as possible, so that he does not become embittered; prison can be a school of virtue only if it provides the prisoner with opportunities of useful employment and intercourse with pleasant companions. Godwin also approves of banishment, provided it is to an unsettled country, where convicts can build up a new society for themselves without interference from the long-corrupted mother country.

Godwin has often been denounced as a visionary, with almost no understanding of human nature; but it seems to me that what he has to say about punishment and coercion is often true, though he puts an extreme case and uses some unconvincing arguments. Leslie Stephen, in his book on *English Thought in the Eighteenth Century*, treats Godwin as an abstract philosopher whose ignorance of human nature leads him into every kind of absurdity. I think that Sir Leslie Stephen has allowed his sturdy common sense to get the better of him. It is interesting to see that Tolstoy's opinions, in this as in many other matters, are almost the same as Godwin's. Did the world's greatest novelist know nothing of human nature?[1]

---

[1] Knowledge of human nature is indispensable to the social philosopher, but of itself it takes him only a little way towards the understanding of social problems. Besides, it was the strength of their emotions and not the weakness of their understandings that led Godwin and Tolstoy astray.

Godwin thought that all positive law is pernicious. Every human predicament differs from every other; every case, therefore, is a rule to itself. To try to fit it to the Procrustean bed of the law is not merely to do violence to justice but is also to limit reason. Positive laws are mechanical standards to which men conform to save themselves the trouble of discovering how justice requires them to act in particular cases. 'The true principle which ought to be substituted in the room of law is that of reason exercising an uncontrolled jurisdiction upon the circumstances of the case.'[1] Godwin's attitude to law and to the legal profession is again very like Tolstoy's, as anyone can see who reads the description of the trial of the prostitute Maslova in *Resurrection*. What Godwin does not understand is that positive laws are not all of them attempts to supersede, nor yet to interpret, 'the dictates of an eternal justice'. Abstract principles of justice will not suffice to tell us how we ought to behave in particular cases; we must have a great deal of other information as well. This Godwin does not deny. But he does not understand that this other information cannot be in the possession of every member of society; nor yet, were it all in everyone's possession, would everyone draw similar inferences from it. In order that large numbers of people should be able to live together, it is necessary that certain uniformities of behaviour should exist among them. But they cannot all of them be expected to arrive, independently, at the knowledge of what those uniformities should be. Regulations must be made by some one; there must be, in every society, some people who collect and analyse the relevant information and then propose uniformities of behaviour. It is one thing to say that obedience to rules ought not to be imposed by force; but it is quite another to say that no rules ought to be made.

Godwin looks forward to the disappearance of all government. 'With what delight,' he says in his book,[2] 'must every well-informed friend of mankind look forward to the auspicious period, the dissolution of political government, of that brute engine which has been the only perennial cause of the vices of mankind, and which . . . has mischiefs of various sorts incorporated with its substance, and no otherwise to be removed than by its utter annihilation!' But

[1] Bk. VII, ch. viii.   [2] Bk. V, ch. xxiv.

he does not advocate the immediate destruction of government, for the very vices that are the products of government make it necessary that there should be some coercion, and therefore some government to apply it. It is only after much time has elapsed and when at last truth reigns supreme in all men's minds that governments will be unnecessary.

But Godwin will have it that the vices they engender cannot be cured by governments. The progress of truth, which is to say the rational education of mankind, is a task for which governments are peculiarly unsuited.

Governments are the causes of most evils. Some of these evils, on occasions much less frequent than they suppose, they are able to prevent. But to cure any of them is quite beyond their power. The great instrument of governments is force, which, though it can sometimes prevent evil, can never destroy its causes in the minds of men. Force, indeed, must always create some evil, not only because it inflicts pain but also because those who suffer it are debased and made vindictive. It is reason alone that can get at the roots of evil; and governments, expert in the use of force, cannot know how to promote reason. Godwin's final verdict on government is that we should put up with as little of it as possible until we can get rid of it altogether, for it is always liable to do much evil and can only prevent a small amount.

Godwin was a communist. 'He who looks at his property with the eye of truth,' he says,[1] 'will find that every shilling of it has received its destination from the dictates of reason.' If you have a shilling in your pocket, which your neighbour says he needs, then, if that neighbour is speaking the truth and your own need is not greater, that shilling belongs to him; and if you keep it in your pocket, you are robbing him. But if each man has a claim to his neighbour's superfluities, does it not follow that, if the claim is allowed, the lazy will become parasites on the industrious? Godwin's answer to this objection is that, if property were equally distributed and men lived simple lives, labour would be so gentle a burden as to be a form of relaxation. He estimates that one-twentieth of England's inhabitants could produce all the food and all the other necessaries required by them all; so that, if all luxury were abolished and everybody worked, no one would need to work

[1] Bk. VIII, ch. i.

more than half-an-hour a day. It was possible for men of good will to take this estimate seriously in an unstatistical age.

Godwin, unlike the communists and socialists of to-day, disliked co-operation. All co-operation, because it forces men to suit each other's convenience, restricts their liberty. Some co-operation is unavoidable, but he thinks that, if men take care to reduce their needs to a minimum, they will contrive to satisfy most of them without co-operation. Above all else, Godwin disliked the sort of co-operation which involves cohabitation and marriage. 'So long as I seek to engross one woman to myself and to prohibit my neighbour from proving his superior desert and reaping the fruits of it, I am guilty of the most odious of all monopolies.'[1]

So much, then, for the more important of Godwin's doctrines. Except for some few fundamental principles, he had little enough in common with the utilitarians who preceded him. Nor was he destined to have much influence on his utilitarian successors, with the possible exception of John Stuart Mill. Many of the arguments with which Godwin defends the exercise of private judgment are strikingly similar to those used by the younger Mill in *Liberty*. Both men make the same assumptions: that the prevalence of truth is beneficial to mankind and that it will best prevail in those societies in which no attempt is made to restrain the individual's private judgment. There is good evidence for the truth of the second of these two assumptions, but not much for the first. Apart from John Stuart Mill, two other important European thinkers preached doctrines in important respects similar to those of Godwin. I mean Proudhon and Tolstoy but, so far as I know, there is no reason to believe that they were either of them directly influenced by their English precursor.[2]

[1] Bk. VIII, ch. vi.
[2] Though Tolstoy read *Political Justice*, he did not derive his opinions from it.

CHAPTER VI

JAMES MILL

1. HIS IMPORTANCE

THE radical utilitarianism that had a great influence on the course of
English history was the creation, not of Godwin, but of Bentham
and James Mill. It repudiated nothing more vigorously than anar-
chism and communism. It was the creed of men who believed in
private property and the efficient punishment of malefactors.

James Mill has been called the disciple of Bentham, although
from the first years of their acquaintance he influenced his master
almost as much as he was influenced by him. Mill was an admirer
of Bentham, but he was also the sterner and more vigorous character;
and he could not admire without irritating as well. Yet Bentham's
debt to Mill is a great one. It was Mill who helped him to commit
himself irrevocably to the democratic cause; and it was Mill who
transmitted his doctrines to other minds, giving a more popular
and vigorous expression to them than Bentham could have done.
Bentham was always a hard worker, and he needed no Scottish
disciple, however stern and energetic, to keep him at work. But
he had never known how to present his doctrines in a form attractive to the general reader. James Mill was useful to Bentham, as
the Genevan Dumont had been, as a man who could stimulate him
not only to write but to publish, and who could help him to make
what he wrote fit for publication. But Mill was a much abler man
than Dumont; and indeed, in some ways, he was abler than Bentham
himself. He was the more acute and the more rigorous logician;
and he had a better knowledge of economics than his master.

No one denied more energetically than Mill that Bentham had
disciples. He said that only two men with any pretension to letters
enjoyed the intimacy of Bentham and had the opportunity to learn
much from him. Neither of these men, according to Mill (who was
one of them), was of the sort who could take any man for a master,
'though they were drawn to Mr. Bentham by the sympathy of
common opinions, and by the respect due to a man who had done

97

more than anybody else to illustrate and recommend doctrines, which they deemed of first class importance to the happiness of mankind.'[1] Though Mill would not be a disciple, history has decided that he was one and that he served his master well. Though it may be misleading to talk of a School of Benthamites, it is plausible to do so only because James Mill was so vigorous and influential an exponent of Bentham's doctrines.

Indeed, it was James Mill who made Benthamism both influential and unpopular; and it needed a stern and vigorous Scotsman to do both these things at once. For the Benthamites, or Philosophic Radicals, were certainly not popular. They were too radical and too fond of theory to please the Whigs, who were willing to make some reforms but would not be bullied into accepting simple principles and drawing extreme conclusions from them. The Whig attitude to the Benthamites was best expressed by Macaulay, in his articles in the *Edinburgh Review*, where he castigated them all but none more vigorously than James Mill. Macaulay believed that his blows were damaging but in a dispute about first principles he was no match for Mill. Yet he did not feel at a disadvantage, for there are persons who imagine themselves at home everywhere, however little they know the place in which they find themselves.

The Benthamites were also disliked by such popular radicals as Cobbett and Hunt, whom Mill despised, though they did more than any other men to frighten the ruling oligarchy into passing the first Reform Bill. Mill thought little better of Cartwright and Sir Francis Burdett, but he was not above giving them advice. Among the popular radicals, he made an exception only in favour of Francis Place, who was neither an orator nor a journalist, but a patient organizer always willing to listen to his intellectual superiors.

That the great Reform Bill was passed through Parliament was largely owing to the efforts of three sets of people, who none of them liked the others. The radical agitators, the Whigs, and the Benthamites all made their separate contributions to the common victory. But the contribution of the Benthamites, though it was great, was the least important of the three. The Whigs saw the great measure through Parliament, while the agitators frightened their opponents into acquiescence. The role of the Benthamites was to irritate and stimulate the Whigs, and to restrain the popular

[1] *Fragment on Mackintosh*, p. 124. (1870 edition.)

radicals as far as their influence could reach them. For the Benthamites, like all reasonable men who wish well to mankind, hated violent revolution.

The Benthamites served their country best after the passage of the great Reform Bill. Though Bentham died in 1832 and James Mill only four years later, their doctrines were most influential in the small but powerful circles of practical intellectuals who, in all civilized countries, make the subordinate decisions of policy that are hardly less important than the major ones. If the ideas and the spirit of Bentham were long active in these circles, to which Britain owes so many of her greatest reforms, this was due, above all, to James Mill.

2. HIS THEORY OF MORALS

When we leave Bentham's discussion of first principles to notice the use he makes of them, we pass from darkness into light. It was left to James Mill to describe clearly what his master could only hint at. Mill's theory of morals is to be found in two of his works, in the last nine chapters of the second volume of the *Analysis of the Phenomena of the Human Mind* and in the *Fragment on Mackintosh*. It is the first complete and clearly-stated utilitarian moral philosophy which is very different from that of Hume. Where Paley is summary and Bentham confused, Mill is both elaborate and clear. His reputation has probably suffered on that account, for it is often easy to trace his errors to their source. He puts his inadequate views so vigorously that his reader is left in no doubt that the means are lacking to make a true theory. And if he later introduces the very notions he has excluded, the manoeuvre is too obvious to pass unnoticed.

Mill's theory of morals is part of an attempt to explain all the phenomena of the human mind in terms of the association of sensations and ideas, which are the mere copies of sensations. Since this attempt cannot succeed, Mill is sometimes obliged, though he does not know it, to abandon his own definitions and to use words in their ordinary meanings. But though his definitions and his uses of words do not always coincide, his meaning is usually clear enough. Or if he is confused, it is easier with him than with most men to detect the nature of the confusion.

Mill distinguishes between interesting and indifferent sensations, between those that are pleasant or painful and those that are neither. The idea of a pleasant sensation he calls a desire, and the idea of a painful one, an aversion. Though his theory of the association of ideas cannot explain how men come to conceive of the past and the future, Mill believes that it can, and therefore makes full use of the distinction between them. 'The word desire,' he says, 'is commonly used to mark the idea of a pleasurable sensation, when the Future is associated with it.'[1]

Mill then goes on to distinguish between desire and motive. He says that when the idea of a future pleasant sensation is associated with the idea of our own action as its cause, then we have a motive. But not every motive leads to action, for we can have several motives at the same time, and the action prompted by one of them makes it impossible for the others to produce their effects. That education is best which creates such habits in men that the motives leading to actions having the best consequences are usually victorious.

Like Bentham, Mill makes the morality of an action depend not on the agent's motive but on his intention. The motive of an action is the idea of those of its pleasurable consequences for whose sake it is done, and its intention is all of its consequences expected by the agent. An intention, according to Mill, is immoral whenever a man acts expecting a preponderance of evil consequences or without caring whether there will be such a preponderance or not. For James Mill, as for Bentham, the man of virtue is the good calculator. 'The men, therefore, philosophers they ought not to be called, who preach a morality without calculation, take away morality altogether; because morality is an attribute of intention; and an intention is then only good when the act intended has in the sum of its ascertainable consequences a superiority of good over evil.'[2] Mill says that the rightness of an action is the same thing as its utility. His meaning may, perhaps, be more precisely expressed if it is said that a man acts rightly whenever the expected consequences of what he does are better than those of any other action possible to him.

Mill still has to explain how it is that men come to act morally. For the mere opinion that of several actions possible under the

---

[1] *Anal. Hum. Mind*, II, ch. xix, p. 153.   [2] *Fragment on Mackintosh*, p. 164.

circumstances one will have better consequences than any of the others is no motive for doing it. Mill's explanation of why men act morally is a simple one. Every man, if left to himself, would seek his own pleasures without regard for other people's. But no man is left to himself and men have to learn by experience to live comfortably together. It is experience that teaches them, out of their innumerable actions, to select one class they call moral and another they call immoral. Those actions are moral which it is important to other men that each man should do but which he has no interest in doing; and those actions are immoral which it is important to other men that he should not do but from which he has no interest in abstaining. Men provide each other with motives for doing moral actions and abstaining from immoral ones. They see to it that good comes to him who does the former and abstains from the latter, and evil to him who abstains from the former and does the latter. They can do this either by punishing and rewarding, or merely by praising and blaming. Experience will decide what means are best suited to the purpose. 'The whole business of the moral sentiments,' says Mill, 'moral approbation and disapprobation, has this for its object, the distribution of the good and evil we have at command, for the production of acts of the useful sort, the prevention of acts of the contrary sort.'[1]

This theory so far combines elements borrowed from Hobbes and from Hume and adds others suggested by Bentham. Unlike Hobbes, James Mill calls that action right which leads to the greatest possible happiness, no matter whose. But like Hobbes, he believes that every man naturally desires only his own happiness and must be supplied artificially with selfish motives for promoting other people's. And in the supply of these motives, he ascribes an important role to the moral sentiments. His description of these sentiments and of the manner in which they arise in us takes Mill a long way from Hobbes. For he admits that, though the original distinction between moral and immoral actions is due to men's reflection about what it is in their interest that other men should do, the habit of moral action is acquired by all men long before they are capable of justifying it rationally. According to Mill, we acquire the moral habit in this way: our parents praise some actions and blame others, and they reward us for doing the former and

[1] Ibid., p. 250.

punish us for doing the latter; we therefore associate the idea of praise with one class of actions and of blame with another, and to do this is to have the notions of praiseworthy and blameworthy actions. Since we desire the usual consequences of the former and avoid those of the latter, we soon acquire the habit of moral action, which later remains with us even when we are no longer liable to suffer these consequences.

This process, as Mill describes it, would appear to lead mankind away from the selfish hedonism natural to them in their primitive state to what is at least the threshold of true morality. For if, the moral habit once acquired, a man does the praiseworthy actions and abstains from the blameworthy ones, even when he no longer expects either praise or blame, is he not capable of unselfishness, of action prompted by some idea not of a pleasurable sensation to be experienced by himself? But Mill will not let mankind attain virtue at so cheap a price. He has an argument, and a most un-plausible one, to show that men are completely selfish after all. The man who does a praiseworthy action, when he knows that he will receive not praise but blame for it, still acts in anticipation of praise. This anticipation is only momentary, but it is so powerful that it can, though immediately succeeded by the expectation of evil, take effect in virtuous action. A momentary idea can, says Mill, have the strongest effect upon us, however quickly other ideas succeed it. To deserve praise is to anticipate it. Mill can give no other meaning to the notion of desert. A man, therefore, who is eager to deserve praise when he knows he cannot get it, must, if only for a moment, expect it and then come to know that his expectation is vain. The absurdity of this argument is evident, even if we accept Mill's premises. To anticipate anything is, in his view, to have an idea of it associated with the idea of its cause. If what a man anticipates is pleasant and its cause is his own action, then, unless there is something to prevent its doing so, his anticipation must produce that action. But in the case in question, there is something to prevent its doing so; there is the subsequent anticipation of evil. And this latter anticipation must either replace the former or, if they co-exist, it must be the stronger, for otherwise it is impossible, within the limits of James Mill's philosophy, to explain what is meant by the statement that the man does the praiseworthy action though he expects to be blamed for it.

Mill's account of sympathy and benevolence is no more satisfactory than his account of virtue. 'The idea', he tells us, 'of a man enjoying a train of pleasures, or happiness, is felt by every body to be a pleasurable idea. The idea of a man under a train of sufferings or pains, is equally felt to be a painful idea. This can arise from nothing but the association of our own pleasures with the first idea, and of our pains with the second. We never feel any pains and pleasures but our own. The fact, indeed, is, that our very idea of the pains or pleasures of another man is only the idea of our own pains, or our own pleasures, associated with the idea of another man.'[1] No man as intelligent as James Mill undoubtedly was ever produced a worse argument than this. The association of ideas, as he conceives it, cannot explain how we come by the notion of any man, ourself or another. But since we do come by the notion of another man, how can it be impossible for us to have an idea of his pleasures or pains? For, on Mill's theory, our idea of another man can be nothing but our idea of a train of feelings not our own. And what could be more absurd than his statement that our idea of another man's pleasure is the idea of our own associated with our idea of him? Who can doubt that when I think of my own pleasure and of another man, I am still far from thinking of his pleasure? I cannot possibly think of a pleasure as another man's, if I continue to think of it as my own. It is Mill himself, though he often warns us to beware of the intricacies of language, who has been caught.

Whenever he feels most open to attack, Mill resorts to his doctrine of the indissoluble association of ideas. Speaking of himself, he says that 'it is Mr. Mill who first made known the great principle of the indissoluble association. It is he, who has shewn, that various mental phenomena, which had puzzled all preceding inquirers, may be satisfactorily accounted for, by application to them of the principle of indissoluble association'.[2] He uses the principle when he wishes to show that something is there, though other people have not noticed it. Whenever, because they have been so often repeated together in the past, the association between two or more ideas is so strong that they always arise in our minds in such close combination as not to be distinguishable, there is an indissoluble association between them. The unreflecting mind, when it has these associated ideas, mistakes the complex whole presented to it

[1] *Anal. Hum. Mind*, II, ch. xxi, p. 175. [2] *Fragment on Mackintosh*, p. 173.

for a simple one. To illustrate his meaning, Mill offers the analogy
of a wheel, on which seven colours have been painted, but which
revolves so rapidly that it looks white. In like manner, several
ideas, passing quickly through the mind, appear to be one; and the
consequence is that men have come to mistake many of their
complex ideas for simple ones. Among such complex ideas mistaken
for simple ones are most of the notions that the moral philosopher
must analyse. It is no wonder, then, that James Mill should believe
that the discoverer of the principle of indissoluble association could
make the greatest progress in this analysis. He thinks that 'Mr. Mill
(has) traced home to their source, not one, but all of the social
affections; and (has) shown by distinct analysis that they are entirely
composed of pleasurable feelings'.[1]

Now, Mill's analogy can help no one to understand his meaning.
It is no more than a manner of speaking to say that the colour
white is composed of seven others; it is either an elliptical statement
about the physical causes of our sensations of colour or it is a statement about the order in which those sensations succeed one another.
When we look at what is white, the colour that we see is as simple as
any other. We do not see seven colours in such rapid succession
that we cannot distinguish between them and then mistake them for
what appears to be an eighth colour but does not in fact exist.
If virtue and the social affections are related to our ideas of our
own pleasures and pains as white is to the seven prismatic colours,
then, whatever their causal connexion with these pleasures and
pains, they differ in kind from them. Moreover, James Mill has no
right to talk of sensations or ideas succeeding one another so rapidly
that they are indistinguishable. For he says that to have a sensation
is to know that one has it, and to have two sensations is to know
they are two.[2] His own conception of the nature of knowledge for-
bids any other conclusion. Nothing, on his theory, can ever be
indistinguishable from anything else. But what cannot be done in
the unaccommodating world is possible in the world of philosophy,
where a man can cut the ground from under his own feet and yet
stand upon it.

James Mill, like Bentham, takes pride in the fact that his theory
provides an objective standard of morality. In what does this
objectivity consist? If Mill is saying no more than that he intends to

[1] Ibid., p. 188.　　　[2] *Anal. Hum. Mind*, I, ch. v, p. 170, and II, ch. xiv, p. 10.

use the word *right* as if it meant *useful*, his statement is unimportant. If he is saying that the English habitually use the two words in the same meaning, his statement is disputable. But even if we suppose it true, we are no nearer to an objective standard of morality. For if *right* means *useful*, it is clear that it cannot mean *morally obligatory*. When, therefore, he has to explain how men come to regard some actions as morally obligatory, Mill has no alternative but to follow the example of Hume and have recourse to the moral sentiments. He does, it is true, insist that men only approve what they believe to be useful. But this is also, though with some qualifications that Mill would reject, the opinion of Hume. Yet Mill believes that his system is superior to Hume's because it provides an objective standard of morality. His purpose in the *Fragment on Mackintosh* is to defend this standard against the man whom he considers the most impertinent of its critics.

3. His Political Theory

The elder Mill's political theory is even simpler than his system of morals. Its fundamental principles are expounded in an article on *Government* published in the 1820 edition of the *Encyclopaedia Britannica*.

Government, according to Mill, deals with a particular class of pleasures and pains, those that men derive from one another. Now, the means to happiness are not naturally abundant, and men must work to produce them. But most work is unpleasant; and since all men desire pleasure and avoid pain, they will try, unless they are prevented, to seize the fruits of other men's labour and to do nothing themselves. Mill believes that it is a law of human nature that every man desires as much power as will enable him to make the persons and properties of other men subservient to his pleasures. It is therefore desirable, if the means of happiness are to be produced in the greatest abundance, that every man should retain as much as possible of the fruits of his labour. But this he can only do if all men unite together and delegate to some few of their number the power to protect them all. Those who exercise this protective power are the government.

How can the many ensure that the few will use this power to protect them? Since it is a law of human nature that every man

H

desires to make other men subservient to his pleasures, there is a constant danger that the governors will abuse their power, making those whom they ought to protect their victims. There exists only one device which can always prevent this abuse of power. This device is representative government, which makes the governors responsible to the governed; for though all the members of a community cannot govern, they can choose the persons who do. Thus it is that James Mill, starting from the same premises as Hobbes, arrives at the conclusion that the best of all governments is a representative democracy. His theory is the same as Bentham's, but expressed more simply and with greater vigour.

Writing for an educated public still hostile to radical ideas, James Mill is careful not to offend too many prejudices. Though Bentham had advocated a unicameral legislature and had quietly assumed that the properly constituted state would be a republic, Mill attacks neither the monarchy nor the House of Lords. He says only that if, as their supporters say, kings and legislators by right of birth are necessary institutions, no representative assembly, whose interests are those of the nation, will wish to abolish them. Such an evasive argument comes very properly from a utilitarian anxious to avoid a controversy more likely to cause offence than to lead to useful results. Even Bentham, a scholarly recluse bearing the reactions of the public very little in mind, had known that to abolish monarchy and aristocracy in England was not practical politics. James Mill, in theory as little as Bentham a friend of mixed government, is writing to convince a hostile public and so makes known to them only those of his opinions he is most anxious they should share.

Nor does James Mill advocate universal suffrage but only a franchise so wide that it will make impossible the predominance of sinister interests. He does not tell us just how wide it should be to effect this purpose. All that he does is to give us a general rule: that no class of persons ought to be unrepresented whose interests are not obviously included in those of other people. To illustrate his rule, Mill takes the example of children. Their interests, he thinks, are included in those of their parents, who love and take care of them. So, too, the interests of women are largely included in those of their men-folk. But Mill does not think this a sufficient reason for refusing the vote to women. Children are not only loved and cared for by their parents; they are also incapable of knowing their own interests. We may therefore conclude from what Mill says that, though other limitations may be justified in particular circumstances, the universally valid rule is that only those classes ought to be unrepresented whose interests, which they are themselves incapable of promoting, are included in those of other people. The always sufficient reason for refusing the vote to anyone is that, while he cannot himself make a rational use of it, there is someone else, whose interest includes his own, who can.

James Mill admits that most people do not know their own interests. But he thinks this no reason for excluding them from the franchise. A narrow ruling class will, he thinks, always act badly, because they will prefer their own interests to those of the public. This is an inevitable consequence of the incurable selfishness of mankind.[1] However wise or foolish an oligarchy may be, they will never promote the greatest happiness of the greatest number, for the interests of the entire community are never included in those of any small class within it. But the ignorance of the multitude can be cured or, rather, it can always be diminished. The best way of promoting the public happiness is to enfranchise the many and to educate them; and, in any case, it is a better way than to leave government to the irresponsible few, whatever their wisdom. It may be difficult and expensive to educate the masses, but it is impossible to prevent a small ruling class from promoting their own happiness at the expense of other people.

The case for representative democracy has seldom been put with such economy and vigour. We may believe, to-day, that ignorance is harder to cure than Mill thought it was, but we would most of us, in Western Europe and North America, agree with him when he says that no irresponsible ruling class can be trusted to govern in the interest of the whole community. Indeed, we have evidence of the truth of this more terrible than Mill ever knew. The greatest oppressors have seized power by exploiting the hatreds of the people but they have not been responsible to them. The power

[1] When Mill, in this context, speaks of men's selfishness, he is not thinking of his own analysis of virtue, benevolence and all the social affections into 'indissoluble' associations of a man's ideas of his own pleasures with his ideas of other people as their causes. As Mill himself says, whatever the analysis of the social affections, they remain what they are. When he talks of the selfishness of men's political behaviour, he uses the word in its ordinary meaning as a thing different from benevolence, gratitude, and all the social affections.

of governments and the discipline of organized minorities is such that there never was a time when oppressors could afford to be so indifferent to the reactions of their victims. This sort of oppression, of which Mill knew nothing, does not exist in primitive and illiterate communities. It is to be found only in parts of the world that are considerably industrialized, where schools are many and political doctrines imported from the West prevail. It is therefore the product of the same conditions that make possible modern representative democracy. But this in no way weakens but rather adds to the strength of Mill's arguments. There was a time when representative government was impossible everywhere. Men could not do otherwise than submit to rulers who oppressed them, but the very conditions that made responsible government impossible placed some limits on men's power to oppress one another. But among European peoples to-day, responsible government (however difficult) is not impossible, while oppressors have opportunities unknown before.

We may qualify Mill's arguments in many ways and yet find in them a powerful support for democracy. Natural differences of ability, which education cannot abolish, are much greater than he supposed, but it is not easy to distinguish the wise from the foolish. The small minority of clever men do not form a separate class with common interests, and it is not possible to segregate them and to make irresponsible governors of them. There is no argument against democracy from the stupidity of mankind, unless it can be shown that most governments are so much wiser than their subjects, that the latter have less to fear from their selfishness than to gain from the unfettered exercise of their wisdom. In primitive communities, where knowledge is scarce and the effective use of power difficult, there is a case against democracy. It can be argued that what little knowledge is there to be had must be the monopoly of a small class, since the means are lacking of distributing it more widely; and that the people, being ignorant, would do well not to meddle with what they cannot understand. But the same causes, industrial progress and the accumulation of wealth, which make it possible to diminish popular ignorance, also increase the power of governments to oppress their subjects. Representative democracy, from a doubtful good, becomes the only alternative to the worst of political evils. Mill, with no experience to guide him, could say nothing about the defects of the system he advocated. He looked upon it as an almost perfect device; and it was left to his son to criticize it. John Stuart Mill, compared with some others, was a mild critic of the democracy whose coming he foresaw and which is now with us. To-day, we can bring more formidable accusations against it than any he could think of, and yet we have better cause to defend it than any earlier generation.

CHAPTER VII

UTILITARIANISM AND THE CLASSICAL ECONOMISTS

THE political theory of Bentham and the elder Mill derives, through Hume, from Hobbes. Like all the other utilitarians they assume that, outside the narrow circle of his family and friends, most of a man's actions of which other men need take notice are designed to obtain some advantage for himself. Hobbes had said nothing to suggest that the public happiness is itself desirable, but he had shown that men can turn each other's selfishness to good account, that every man can find it his interest to live in a society in which all men, himself included, are often obliged to do what they do not want or to refrain from what they do. In the state of nature men interfere with one another, and this interference makes their lives intolerable. They therefore set up a political society, which substitutes a milder, more orderly and economical interference for the repeated, brutal and incalculable shocks to which they were previously exposed. Like a house in which travellers shelter from the storm, society protects men much more than it limits their freedom. When Hobbes talked of an absolute sovereign, he meant only that the extent of his powers must be determined by himself; he did not mean that the sovereign must control all the activities of his subjects. Within the wide limits of his country's laws, each man governs himself. When Hobbes lived, governments made few laws and men still oppressed each other more than they were oppressed by their governments.

But Hobbes gave mankind no advice about the proper extent of a sovereign's power. He prescribed no rules to guide the sovereign in deciding when it was his own and his subjects' interest that the laws should be silent. It was Mandeville, in his *Fable of the Bees*, who first taught modern Europeans that there exists a natural harmony of interests in the economic sphere. The greater the variety of men's wants, the easier for every man to find it his private interest to produce what will satisfy some of these wants.

110

The more acquisitive men are, the more intent on pleasure and refinements of pleasure, the easier it is for them to co-operate. As society grows richer, its members are drawn closer together, each of them dependent for his happiness on an always greater number of the others. But the more men find it their interest to work peacefully together, the less it is necessary to oblige them to do so. Mandeville did not isolate men's activities as producers and distributors of material wealth, and say that with these activities governments ought not to interfere. But though he did not draw this conclusion it is implied by his theory.

Mandeville's argument, differently put so that it might convince without annoying, was adopted by Hume and by his friend and admirer, Adam Smith. Hume advocated a greater freedom of trade than existed in his day, and exposed some of the fallacies to which governments were still attached. But it was Adam Smith who described the economic processes whereby the natural harmony of interests is assured. The processes that he described are not the inventions of governments; they arise naturally in all societies as men learn to use their labour and skill more effectively for the satisfaction of their wants.

The classical economists, especially the three most famous of them, Adam Smith, Malthus and Ricardo, were utilitarians. They believed that the proper end of government is the greatest happiness of the governed. They were most of them practical men. They did not write books on economics merely because they were interested in describing how men produce and distribute material wealth. They were great controversialists in their day, and what they wanted above all was to give advice to governments. They called the science, whose creation is ascribed to them and to the French physiocrats, political economy. The advice they gave was mostly negative, but the principle behind it was utilitarian. They said to the government: don't do what we tell you not to do and men will be the happier for your abstinence; you need only look at the methods whereby they produce and exchange goods and services (and we have taken the trouble to describe these methods for you) and you will see that we are right. The classical political economy, which prevailed in this country from 1776 until the middle of the next century, was the theory behind the advice given by utilitarians to the successive governments of their country.

As they all gave different advice, they quarrelled about the theory and so were obliged to take more notice of each other than the government took of them. But for all that, their first object, as Professor Cannan has shown, was practical.

1. ADAM SMITH

In his *Theory of the Moral Sentiments*, Adam Smith, as became the disciple of Hume, had allowed a large role to sympathy. But in the *Wealth of Nations* he assumes that man, the producer and distributor of material wealth, is completely selfish. Nevertheless, the general economic interest is secure, because, though it is the object of no man's endeavour, it is the natural result of the division of labour and the mechanism of exchange. These two devices ensure that each man does what he is best fitted to do, and that he is more than compensated for the unpleasantness of his work by the utility of the objects he can acquire as a result of it. 'The real price of everything, he tells us, 'what everything really costs to the man who wishes to acquire it, is the toil and trouble of acquiring it . . . Labour was the first price that was paid for all things.'[1] His theory is that all economic activity is the endurance of present pain in the hope of future pleasure to be got by consuming the fruits of one's labour or what is exchanged for them. The division of labour and the market ensure, between them, that as much as possible of what is useful is produced at the least cost in terms of labour. Whatever impedes the division of labour and the free operation of the market is therefore injurious; for the division of labour ensures that a given amount of work, and therefore also of pain, produces as much as possible of what is useful, while it is owing to the market that useful things are produced in the order of their utility and get to the people who want them

Even if we accept the psychological and utilitarian assumptions on which it rests, Adam Smith's argument is plausible only when one all-important qualification is made. What he says may be true, provided that natural resources, however scarce, are available to everyone on the same terms as to anyone else. As this has never been the case in any society we know of, all that Adam Smith is entitled to say is that the division of labour and the free market

[1] *Wealth of Nations*, Bk. I, ch. iv.

produce the greatest amount of happiness compatible with the existing system of property. Adam Smith was, of course, quite aware that the unequal distribution of property enables the owners of scarce resources to charge a rent for their use, which they can spend to buy the produce of other men's labour without needing to produce anything themselves. But he did not allow this fact to weaken his belief in the natural harmony of interests.

Even if we suppose (though they are not to be found in the *Wealth of Nations*) that there are solid utilitarian arguments for the inequality of property, there are still passages enough in that work to disturb our faith in the natural harmony of interests. Adam Smith says that with the progress of civilization real wages will increase and profits decrease, which suggests that there may be a conflict of interests between labourers and capitalists. It does not follow that there is one, for the incomes of individual capitalists may continue to rise though the return on each unit of their capital falls. And even if their combined share of the national income should come to be a smaller fraction of it, which it need not do though the rate of interest falls, its absolute amount may be much greater. These are matters that require proof, if the doctrine of the natural harmony of interests is to be saved. But Adam Smith is content to say nothing about them. He also tells us that rents will increase with real wages, so that (given the system of property, and its justice unquestioned) there is an apparent harmony of interests between landowners and labourers. And in another placehe says that labourers seldom know their own interests and that land-owners are lazy and improvident. The capitalists, on the other hand, are the best informed, most intelligent and most industrious class in the community. In the system of Adam Smith, it is they that are the real makers of progress. It is a curious harmony of interests which appears to increase the rewards of the ignorant and the lazy more quickly than those of the intelligent and industrious. Smith's position can perhaps be defended, but its truth is not obvious. It may be that the capitalists, even though the balance of advantages should turn against them, have more to gain than to lose from the uncontrolled progress of material civilization. But it does not follow that they can do nothing to redress the balance. Could they not improve their relative position by acquiring control of the government and having laws made in their favour? Is it certain that, if they could do so, the general happiness would be diminished? What, after all, does a natural harmony of interests amount to? It is clear that Adam Smith never asked himself these questions. It is not enough to show (what he never did) that every class has something to gain from the community's economic progress; it must also be proved that neither the community as a whole nor any class within it has less to gain by leaving that progress to itself than by seeking to control it. For anything that either Adam Smith or any other economist knew to the contrary, it might be true both that if one class prospers all must do so and that the greatest prosperity of any one class is incompatible with the greatest prosperity of them all. But if this were so, it would be misleading to talk of a natural harmony of selfish interests. Though the greatest happiness of the whole community depended on leaving men's economic activities uncontrolled, every class might stand to gain by using the state to control them in its own exclusive interest.

Adam Smith did not attempt to reconcile his later admissions with the original assumption with which they are not obviously compatible. M. Halévy attributes this failure to his noticing these apparent symptoms of disharmony long after he had made the assumption. As they successively occurred to him, Adam Smith made a note of each of these symptoms, but he never realized that, taken together, they are a serious threat to the position from which he started. He therefore saw no reason why he should abandon or defend that position. But since he retained it, he was led, though unaware of what he was doing, to minimize the importance of every admission that might make it untenable. Halévy compares these admissions with 'foreign bodies that the organism is always trying to eliminate'.[1] He assumes that the theory could not possibly assimilate them, but he goes too far. Halévy would be right if it followed, with no need for further evidence, that where some people stand to gain less than others, it is always their interest not to leave matters alone. He knows just as little as any classical economist what conditions must prevail before there can be a natural harmony of selfish interests.

[1] *The Growth of Philosophic Radicalism*, p. 103.

2. MALTHUS

The next important economist after Adam Smith was Malthus, whose *Essay on Population* first appeared in 1798, twenty-two years after the *Wealth of Nations*. It had been a favourite idea in the eighteenth century, especially in France and America but also in Britain, that the cause of depopulation is luxury. Rich men, it was thought, waste the substance of the community and spread the vices that cause disease and death. We have already noticed one utilitarian clergyman, William Paley, who rejected this idea and put forward the opposite one that poverty increases population, while he defended luxury, saying that it provides work for the poor and keeps them out of mischief. Malthus, another utilitarian clergyman, also rejected the popular theory, but for reasons very different from Paley's. Paley had agreed with those whose theory he rejected that most countries could support much larger populations than inhabited them; he had merely denied that luxury is the cause of depopulation. But Malthus also denied that most countries, and in particular the countries of Western Europe, were under-populated. Population, he said, has a natural tendency to increase at a geometrical ratio, while the means of subsistence will normally increase at no more than an arithmetical ratio. There exists, therefore, in every old-established country a constant pressure of population on the means of subsistence. This is so whether or not there are great inequalities of property. Malthus admitted that in newly discovered continents, before natural resources are fully developed, the means of subsistence may increase fast enough to keep pace with this natural growth of population. But in older countries, where all the better land is already cultivated, this cannot happen. Malthus therefore concluded that, whatever the distribution of property, the greatest part of the inhabitants of all old countries must be wretchedly poor, receiving a subsistence just sufficient to keep them alive. Those born in excess of the number that the resources of the community can maintain are condemned to a premature death by famine or disease. Malthus called misery and vice the positive checks that keep down the population to the level of subsistence; and he also admitted that there is another, which he called moral or preventive, consisting in voluntary abstinence from procreation. But in the first edition of his *Essay*, he did not attach great importance to this moral check.

It may be that when he published the first edition of his *Essay*, Malthus was so anxious to refute the theory that luxury is the cause of depopulation, that he forgot his obligations as a clergyman. He had said vice was a positive check on population. But if population must always grow faster than the means of subsistence, it follows that whatever is needed to check its growth is useful; and if useful, then good. What is called vice is therefore not vice at all, but ought rather to be called virtue. Such a conclusion cannot be avoided if the utilitarian assumptions and the facts alleged by Malthus are both true. But it is a conclusion that a clergyman must, at all costs, avoid. Besides, Malthus was naturally of a benevolent, if rather conservative, temper. In later editions of his *Essay*, he qualified his doctrine, making it less startling, more plausible and more humane. The moral check, he said, is not yet sufficiently effective, but it may well become so if the proper remedy is applied. And this proper remedy is *education*. Now education, if it can teach people to limit the size of their families, can ensure, not merely that population grows no faster than the means of subsistence, but that it grows more slowly. It can therefore provide, not only an effective substitute for misery and vice, but a remedy for poverty itself. Malthus, in the later editions of his *Essay*, looked forward to the day when the population of England might be two or three times as great and yet the labouring classes much better off than they were in his day.

Malthus, like Bernard Shaw, had no eye for the charms of poverty. He looked forward to its abolition, but was no less anxious that the rich should not be plundered. He thought that the ignorance of the poor, and not the luxury of the rich, is the true cause of misery. Educate the poor and they will not only desire to enrich themselves but will discover the means of doing so. Those who saw in luxury the cause of depopulation implied that there is a natural divergence between the interests of the rich and the poor. Malthus's reply denies the implication and asserts that education alone can put the labouring poor in the way of prosperity. The Poor Laws, he thought, merely aggravated the pauperism they were intended to alleviate. Popular education and savings banks, the encouragement of knowledge and of prudence, were his sovereign remedies.

Otherwise men might safely be left to themselves, without interference from their governments.

Initiative and prudence are, so Malthus thought, the most useful social virtues. But they are virtues that flourish only in a stable society, where men can make calculations about the future without fear that the assumptions on which these calculations rest will cease to hold good. He was a supporter of every institution that promotes social stability. Of these, the two most important, in his opinion, are marriage and private property. He believed that they both involve inequality, since property will not encourage initiative and prudence unless a man has the right to enjoy the fruits of his labour and to pass on to his children, after his death, the unconsumed part of them. But though Malthus taught that inequality is indispensable, he also said that it is the main interest of society to improve the lot of the labouring poor. It was their enrichment that would most rapidly increase the public happiness.

3. RICARDO

Adam Smith, who borrowed it from France, introduced the word distribution into English economic theory. But his main interest as an economist was not to discover how the produce of a nation is divided among the classes that make it up. What he most wanted to do was to describe the advantages of the division of labour, and the laws that determine prices. He was interested in wages, profits and rent as the three constituents of prices. It was Ricardo who, according to Professor Cannan, was the first English economist to declare that the main business of his science is to discover what determines the distribution of the nation's produce. Now, the laissez-faire economist who, in an adolescent capitalist society, pays most attention to prices and to the division of labour, can avoid too close an acquaintance with the facts most disturbing to his utilitarian faith. But as soon as his chief interest becomes the distribution of incomes his position is more difficult. Yet Ricardo remained true to the common doctrine that the uncontrolled is the best of all possible economies. His description of it is depressing to read. Like Dr. Pangloss he reached the point where optimism and pessimism are scarcely to be distinguished. His most gloomy prophecies have turned out to be false.

Ricardo described an economy in which real wages tend to fall, profits are progressively reduced until capital accumulation ceases, and only the landlords prosper. There was information enough at hand to enable him to reach quite different conclusions, but he made his own choice and predicted economic stagnation. His great book, the *Principles of Political Economy and Taxation*, was published in 1817, after men had become familiar with Malthus's theories about population and the nature of rent. Ricardo made use of these theories to determine the shares of the national revenue going to landlords and labourers, so that what was left was profits. This method, apparently so convenient, has one great disadvantage. It suggests that the incomes of capitalists are residuary in some sense in which rents and wages are not. Whatever increases rents, or rents and wages together, will then appear to reduce profits. But the hire of capital is a price that enters into costs of production on much the same terms as the wages of labour and the rent of land. Ricardo treated the national revenue as if it were the gross income of a tradesman, who first pays his landlord and his employees and then keeps what is left.

According to Malthus and to Sir Edward West, who arrived simultaneously at more or less similar conclusions, rent is a sort of premium paid by the cultivators to the owners of the more fertile soils. It arises because fertile land is scarce and can produce more than enough to maintain those who cultivate it. When population increases, there is a greater demand for necessaries, land that is less fertile is brought into cultivation and the prices of necessaries rise. Costs of production on the more fertile lands remain the same, but it is the costs on the least fertile that determine prices. The result is that the rent of every piece of land, which is equal to the difference between costs of production on it and on the least fertile land under cultivation, must rise. This simple theory of rent was adopted uncritically by Ricardo. It is only true when three conditions hold good: when the greater demand for necessaries is met by bringing more land into cultivation, when the amount of labour and capital employed on a given quantity of land is not increased, and when there are no great technical improvements that increase productivity. Population might increase and its wants be satisfied by the improved cultivation of a smaller quantity of land; or if some less fertile land were brought into cultivation its crops, more efficiently raised, might be greater than were formerly grown on more fertile soils. Improved cultivation leads, no doubt, to increased rents. But this sort of increase, which is compatible with lower prices, higher real wages and higher profits, did not attract Ricardo. What he needed, to establish his theory, was an increase in rents, together with rising prices, stationary or even falling real wages, and declining profits. Ricardo knew, as well as anyone, that great technical improvements had been made and that more were to be expected. He knew also that the amount of capital sunk into land was much greater than it had been and would, in all probability, still increase. He admitted that these factors must moderate the trends he described, but that they might more than offset them he would not acknowledge. And even this admission was an afterthought. Of the currents, whose flow and counterflow the economist must study, he chose to take special notice of some and to assume that they are stronger than the others.

Having decided that rents will rise because the cost of producing necessaries must do so, Ricardo found no difficulty in showing that money wages will also rise. Labour has, he thought, a natural price, which is the amount 'necessary to enable the labourers, one with another, to subsist and to perpetuate their race without increase or diminution.' This amount consists of a certain quantity of the necessaries of life, so that if the prices of those necessaries rise, the subsistence wage must rise with them. Now, since the increase in rents has already absorbed the increase in prices, this rise in wages must be at the expense of profits. As more and more land is brought into cultivation, money wages steadily rise until profits are so small that people no longer find it worth their while to save. At this point, economic progress ceases.

In the system of Ricardo, as in that of every other economist of his day, the ultimate cause of economic progress is the accumulation of capital. This accumulation increases the demand for labour, wages rise above the natural level, labourers marry earlier and produce larger families, and wages fall once again to the subsistence level. Ricardo admitted that the natural price of labour, the subsistence wage, is itself liable to change. But he believed that over long periods, whose length he would not estimate, it remains unchanged. A rise in the demand for labour increases its supply, just as a fall reduces it, so that the current rate of wages oscillates round the natural price of labour. Ricardo did not deny that the natural price of labour had increased over the centuries. Nor did he positively assert that it would increase no more. But he also spoke of a natural tendency for real wages to fall. How are we to reconcile these apparently contradictory statements? We can do so only in this way. We must suppose Ricardo to have meant that, whereas wages tend always to remain at the subsistence level, this tendency, in the earlier periods of economic progress, is more than offset by the accumulation of capital. The natural price of labour, the subsistence wage just sufficient, according to prevailing notions, to satisfy essential needs, will rise very slowly. But in later periods, when land that is less and less fertile is brought into cultivation, capital accumulation, far from making possible a slow rise in real wages, does not even suffice to prevent their fall. This fall, though it is resisted by the strong tendency of wages to remain at the subsistence level, is due to the much greater costs of production on less fertile land. In the progressive economy, as depicted by Ricardo, the three important factors are the accumulation of capital, the constant pressure of a growing population on the means of subsistence, and the ever more extensive cultivation of less fertile land. Each of these factors has its appropriate effect: the first tends to increase real wages and the demand for labour, the second to keep real wages at a constant level, and the third to increase money wages, while reducing their real value and causing a rapid fall in the rate of profit. In the early stages of capitalist accumulation, the first factor operates more strongly than the other two, but in the end it is the third that is strongest, and it eventually puts a stop to the economic progress caused by the first.

Ricardo could not say when the course of progress would come to an end. He could not even know that real wages had slowly begun to fall. He could say only that there was a beginning and an end, but the distance covered and that still remained to cover he could not estimate. The natural price of labour, the subsistence wage fixed by custom, might rise in the future as it had in the past, and it might, by the time capital accumulation ceased, have reached a point much higher than its present one. The terms laid down by Ricardo for mankind did not exclude these possibilities. But though he did not deny these things with his lips, pessimism was closer to his heart. To illustrate his arguments, he chose examples in which real wages are made to fall; and he preferred to be guided by his own examples than to look for statistics.[1] He did not even believe, as Malthus did, that education might teach the labouring poor to have smaller families and so relieve the pressure of population on subsistence.

Under the hand of Ricardo, the rock on which the classical economists built their system seems to crumble away. The impetus on which progress depends will, he thinks, eventually spend itself, and by the time it is spent, it will have done most for the idle, less for the industrious, and least for the intelligent. Ricardo's capitalist is like the steward of an estate, who exerts himself to increase its produce only to find that his shiftless master takes an always greater share of it. He continues to exert himself in the hope that his reward, though a smaller part of the whole produce, may yet be larger than it was. But eventually he abandons even this hope and tries to increase his reward at the expense of his labourers, who stubbornly resist his efforts. In the end, knowing that greater exertion must enrich others at his expense, he does no more than is just sufficient to maintain the produce of the estate.

Though he believed that uncontrolled progress must end in stagnation, Ricardo remained true to the doctrine of laissez-faire. Though the pursuit of their selfish interests might bring fewer blessings to mankind than Mandeville and Adam Smith had hoped, it was still the truest wisdom to leave men to their own devices. Though the best is worse than we expected, it is the most that we can reasonably hope for. In this diminished sense, the natural harmony of interests still holds good. But whether, reduced to these proportions, it deserves so grand a name is another question.

We can easily imagine how attractive the wilful pessimism of Ricardo must have been to Marx. He also believed that the capitalist economy is progressive and that its progress must come to an end. But in the place of stagnation he put revolution, and he prophesied a final harmony of interests so perfect that governments would wither away. If he loaded Ricardo's picture with still darker colours, it was because he needed a greater contrast with the glory he reserved for mankind.

[1] As Professor Cannan has shown in his excellent book *Theories of Production and Distribution* (1776–1848).

CHAPTER VIII

JOHN STUART MILL

1. His Importance

IF Hume was the greatest of the utilitarians, John Stuart Mill comes next after him. They had this in common, that neither owed a pure allegiance to the doctrine. Otherwise, the two men could hardly have been more different. Hume nearly always knew what he was about; he was as completely in control of his arguments as any philosopher, discussing the most difficult subjects, has ever been. But Mill was not, in this sense, a master. He was often bewildered by the intricacies of his own thought, unaware of the implications of what he had said and of what still remained to be proved. He could abandon a doctrine the most completely when he thought he was defending it with the greatest warmth. But he was much more than a philosopher who was often confused. He had a mind exceptionally hospitable to good ideas, whatever their source, and sometimes capable of inventing them.

John Stuart Mill was educated by his father, and the stories of his extraordinary intellectual achievements in early childhood have often been repeated. He was more thoroughly educated than it is good for any man to be, and his knowledge had so long a start of his understanding that the latter could never catch up with it. He was also physically weak and emotionally inhibited. He had neither the wilful energy of his father, nor the cool temperament of Bentham and Hume.

John Stuart Mill was born in 1806. In 1823, already more learned than most highly educated men, he was appointed a clerk in India House. Thirty-three years later, in 1856, he became Chief of the Office at a salary of £2,000 a year. But he was opposed to the direct rule of India by the English Crown and Parliament, and so in 1858, at the age of fifty-two and after thirty-five years spent in an office, he retired. He had still fifteen years to live, but his health was broken and he could no longer work as he once had done. His two largest books, his *Logic* and his *Political Economy*, had both been completed long before his retirement. Of the three essays, on which his reputation as a moral and political philosopher chiefly depends, only one, *Liberty*, was completed before his retirement, though his wife's death delayed its publication until 1859.

Sir Leslie Stephen, who liked robust talent, thought that Mill was something of a prig. But his autobiography does not create this impression, unless a man, whatever his modesty, who takes himself too seriously, is to be called a prig. Mill was an exceptionally good man, gentle, candid and generous. He was also tender and affectionate, and, unlike the other great utilitarians, contrived to fall deeply in love. The many virtues of a not very happy but truly modest man have touched the hearts of most people who have studied his writings, though others, more difficult to please, have found him unimaginative and unmasculine. Mill lacked gaiety and ease. He was too gentle to express contempt for other men and too solemn to laugh at them.

Mill's *Liberty* was published in 1859, his *Utilitarianism* and his *Considerations on Parliamentary Government* (now known as *Representative Government*) in 1861. These three essays, written by a sick man in his premature old age, exhibit all his defects as a thinker, his lack of clarity, his inconsistency, and his inability either to accept wholeheartedly or to reject the principles inherited from his father and from Bentham. Mill's good qualities serve to accentuate his defects, for his candour causes him to admit one circumstance after another that cannot be reconciled with the assumptions he starts with. Perhaps the most defective of the three essays is *Utilitarianism*, in which Mill seems to lose control of his arguments at every turn. It is the product of an intelligent and honest but almost exhausted mind. The essay on *Liberty* is much better, though it is not exempt from the author's usual faults. *Representative Government*, less abstract than the other two essays, is therefore not liable to the same reproach, though it is, to the political philosopher, the least interesting of the three.

For all their defects, *Liberty* and *Utilitarianism* are important works. The very candour that obliges Mill to admit so much that is inconsistent with the principles handed down to him by his father and Bentham throws a strong light on the inadequacies of the utilitarian theory. Bentham and the elder Mill had elaborated a narrower and less plausible doctrine than Hume's; and its narrowness was precisely what most recommended it to them. But what had served to concentrate and direct their energies, left their heir frustrated and dissatisfied. He felt the need to take into account many things that his father could safely ignore because they meant nothing to him. But the younger Mill did not know how to break the bonds that held him; he did not even understand that it was necessary to do so. If he was unable to turn a blind eye to facts which experience and other men's books had brought to his notice, he was equally incapable of framing new hypotheses to account for them. In this, he was certainly unimaginative. And this was also his great misfortune as a philosopher. He should have had a narrower or else a more inventive mind. He could have had either without coming any nearer to the truth than he did, but his reputation as a philosopher would have been more enviable. As it is, he was less solid and less assured than his father, while he lacked the powerful imagination that has enabled some philosophers, out of the most varied materials, to build a great system, which, however small its resemblance to the real world, yet appears coherent.

2. *Liberty*

Bentham, during the latter part of his life, like James Mill and his utilitarian friends, had looked upon democracy as the certain cure of all political evils. These evils, they thought, were the effects of the activities of sinister interests, and democracy would make these activities impossible. Hume had set mankind a problem in political arithmetic: how can the interests of the governed be equated with those of the governors? Bentham and James Mill were convinced that they knew the answer, and they neither of them lived long enough to discover their error. Bentham died in 1832, when Britain took her first timid step towards democracy; and four years later James Mill, too, was dead. In those days, democracy only existed in America, and no careful study of it could yet be obtained in England. But by the time the younger Mill wrote his *Liberty* much more was known about democracy, and there were already men in Europe who were alive to its defects. The first and ablest of foreign students of the United States, de Tocqueville, had published his *Democracy in America* in 1835, but it was not till several years later that his work was widely known in

England. Mill, when he read it, was soon convinced that some of
the evils described in it were already in existence in his own country.
He was too much of a realist to believe that democracy could be
avoided, and he was too much his father's son to deplore its coming.
His object, in *Liberty*, is to warn men of democracy's attendant evils
and to show them how they can be diminished.

The rule of all, says Mill, is not the rule of each man by himself,
but the rule of each by the others. The will of the people is the
will of the majority; and this majority may desire to oppress.
Precautions are as much needed against this form of oppression as
against any other. Moreover, quite apart from the oppressions of
governments, there is the tyranny of opinion, which is, perhaps,
even more dangerous. 'Wherever there is an ascendant class, a
large portion of the morality of the country emanates from its class
interests, and its feelings of class superiority.'[1] This is no less true
when the ascendant class is a majority.

Men, says Mill, are naturally intolerant whenever their feelings
are strong. If we now have religious freedom, it is because we are
less concerned with religion. Nor, according to Mill, are the
English greater lovers of liberty than other peoples. They and
their cousins in America are inheritors of the same traditional
suspicion of governments; they are therefore more willing than
other people to defend the individual against the encroachments of
organized power. But the tyranny of opinion is perhaps stronger
among them than elsewhere. This was also the belief of de Tocqueville and of Stendhal, but Mill was the first Englishman to doubt
his fellow-countrymen's love of liberty.

Mill's object in this essay is, he tells us, to assert and defend the
principle that 'the sole end for which mankind are warranted,
individually or collectively, in interfering with the liberty of action
of any of their number, is self-protection. That the only purpose
for which power can be rightly exercised over any member of a
civilised community, against his will, is to prevent harm to others.
His own good, either physical or moral, is not a sufficient warrant.'[2]
But Mill makes it clear that he regards this principle as quite
compatible with his utilitarianism. 'It is proper to state,' he says,
'that I forego any advantage which could be derived to my argument
from the idea of abstract right, as a thing independent of utility.'[3]

[1] *Liberty*, ch. i, ¶ 6.   [2] Ibid., ch. i, ¶ 9.   [3] Ibid., ch. i, ¶ 11.

Mill's position, therefore, as he states it in the first chapter of the essay, is this: In a civilized society, no sane adult is responsible to other persons for any part of his conduct that concerns only himself, for it is not in the real interest of society that he should be so responsible. This is Mill's position, as he originally states it; but it is not the position he defends in the remainder of his essay. Indeed, he gives us only one reason for believing that it is desirable, *on utilitarian grounds*, that men should not be answerable to society for what concerns only themselves. He says that interference with the individual for his own sake is likely, more often than not, to be ill-judged. This is to imply that when we try to prevent one man from harming another, we are more likely to succeed than when we try to prevent him from harming himself. Otherwise, Mill quietly assumes that the utilitarian grounds exist and leaves the matter there. Though he has foregone any advantage to be derived from the idea of abstract right, he does not hesitate to put the burden of proof on whoever would deny his principle. What he is himself concerned to do is not to show that there are good utilitarian grounds for the non-interference he advocates, but to determine the limits of the interference which he regards as permissible. It is in this sense that Mill, in his *Liberty*, in untrue to his professed utilitarian principles. He leaves undone all those things that a utilitarian ought to do, but what he does is as well worth doing as anything he ever attempted.

In the second chapter of the essay, Mill deals with the liberty of thought and discussion. He assumes, in fact though not explicitly, that it is to the advantage of mankind that knowledge should increase among them and should be possessed by as many of them as possible. The notion that some beliefs, whether true or false, are salutary and for that reason ought to be protected, he utterly rejects. The opinion that they are salutary is, he says, as much open to doubt as any other. Mill's argument will easily convince anyone who accepts his initial tacit assumption, that it is, in the long run, to man's advantage to know the truth. But it will not convince anyone who makes the opposite assumption. If I believe very strongly that certain beliefs are salutary, I may be willing to admit not only that they are false but also that I may be wrong in believing they are salutary; but if my belief is strong, I shall think it right to act upon it, though I can still conceive of the possibility of my being mistaken.

Most of our actions are inspired by probable opinions; enforcements and suppressions of belief are actions like any others. If it is said that they alone of all actions are never justified, this is an assertion that is not self-evident but stands in as much need of proof as any other.

Mill is, I think, wrong when he says that 'all silencing of discussion is an assumption of infallibility'.[1] It may be true that men who often silence discussion come, in the end, to believe that they are always right. History and our experience both teach us that nothing persuades a man of his infallibility more effectively than the power, long exercised, of silencing others.

But this is not nearly enough to establish Mill's point. It does not prove that those who exercise the power only occasionally and under the guidance of a powerful tradition make any such assumption. A man may admit his fallibility and may yet, believing the matter to be of the utmost importance, enforce his own opinion and suppress that of others, having no other ground for his action than his belief that he is very probably right and that disaster will follow if another opinion prevails.

Mill thinks he has disposed of this objection when he says that 'there is the greatest difference between presuming an opinion to be true because, with every opportunity for contesting it, it has not been refuted, and assuming its truth for the purpose of not permitting its refutation'.[2] This is his answer to those who say, in the words he has himself put into their mouths, that 'there is no greater assumption of infallibility in forbidding the propagation of error, than in any other thing which is done by public authority on its own judgment and responsibility'.[3] Like most of us, when we speak for our opponents, Mill gains an easy victory. But he also misses the point. He makes his objectors say that even the most ordinary governmental action implies an assumption of infallibility. He then easily shows that it does not, and that to act on an opinion is not to assume it cannot be false. And finally he takes it for granted that ordinary governmental action differs, in this respect, from the suppression of opinion supposed to be pernicious. An objector, better advised than those imagined by Mill, might put his case differently. He might say: granted that many opinions are pernicious (since all actions, bad and good, proceed from opinions), it does not follow, because men are fallible and may

[1] Ibid., ch. ii, ¶ 3. [2] Ibid., ch. ii, ¶ 6. [3] Ibid., ch. ii, ¶ 5.

mistake good for evil, that they are entitled to prevent actions alone and never the opinions from which those actions proceed. There are, no doubt, a number of reasons which make it more expedient to control men's actions than their opinions. It is easier to control actions than opinions, and it is also easier to show that they have pernicious consequences. Moreover, a government can supply men with motives for not doing what their pernicious opinions might otherwise cause them to do. Economy is the true utilitarian explanation of why it is better to control men's actions than their beliefs. But it does not follow that governments ought never to control men's opinions, or that, if they try to do so, they claim to be infallible.

Whatever theoretical reservations we may wish to make, we are most of us, who have been educated in this country, inclined to believe that it is better, in almost every case, to leave men's opinions alone. We live in an exceptionally tolerant society, and most of us are practical sceptics. Many different opinions, most of which (though we know not which) we know must be false, have been presented to us for our inspection. Our beliefs do not greatly excite us and we are seldom inclined to act upon them in order to do other people good which they think evil. Should we, contemptuous of other people's opinions, seek to put our peculiar beliefs into practice, there exist, apart from the state, several benevolent institutions to protect even our children and domestic animals from the consequences. But this is not so in all human societies, and in them the liberal philosophy of John Stuart Mill seems less obviously true. Where opinions are many, unexciting, and seldom acted upon in defiance of the hostility of the probable victims of such action, tolerance is a harmless virtue. But where opinions are few, exciting, and acted upon regardless of the consequences, it is not always unwise (though it may be difficult) to keep errors and half-truths out of the minds of foolish enthusiasts.

If we happen to live in a civilized, tolerant and humane society, we can afford to assume, with Mill, that more will be lost than gained by the suppression of pernicious opinions. We can then admire the arguments with which he fortifies our favourite prejudices. He describes, better than any one has done before or since, the conditions that must exist in any society if knowledge is to grow inside it and to be shared by as many of its members as possible. We must tolerate error, says Mill, because our acquaintance with it will deepen and make more lively our knowledge of the truth. We must avoid even the mildest tyranny of opinion, because clever men, the discoverers of truth, are often timid and even a slight persecution will silence or make hypocrites of them. Should a few great thinkers dare to defy persecution, men of smaller abilities, even if they are brave, will not do so, for they have less independence of thought and cannot resist their environment. The truth on any great practical question is too large for any one mind to contain it, and the adjustment of partial truths to each other takes place, not in the isolation of single minds, but 'by the rough process of a struggle between combatants fighting under hostile banners'.¹ No doubt the struggle does not enlighten the combatants; 'but it is not,' says Mill, 'on the impassioned partisan, it is on the calmer and more disinterested bystander, that this collision of opinions works its salutary effect'.² It is in this second chapter, full of the most excellent liberal arguments, that Mill comes closest to the position taken up by Godwin in *Political Justice*. But Mill, unlike Godwin, advocates anarchy only in the realm of ideas.

It is in the third chapter of *Liberty*, in which he discusses 'individuality, as one of the elements of well-being', that Mill, without knowing it, abandons utilitarianism. In it he makes the un-utilitarian complaint 'that individual spontaneity is hardly recognized by the common modes of thinking as having any *intrinsic* worth, or deserving any regard on its own account'.³ He then mentions with approval the doctrine of 'self-realization' preached by William von Humboldt. 'It really is of importance,' says Mill, 'not only what men do, but also what manner of men they are that do it.'⁴ And he asks, 'what more or better can be said of any condition of human affairs than that it brings human beings themselves nearer to the best thing they can be?'⁵ Nothing could be less utilitarian than the spirit of this question. It did not matter, in the least, to Bentham and James Mill what men are like, whether they are highly developed individuals or 'ape-like imitators', provided only that they are happy, that they have as much pleasure as possible and as little pain. The younger Mill does, as a matter of fact, undertake to show that the highly-developed individual is useful to society;

¹ Ibid., ch. ii, ¶ 36.   ² Ibid., ch. ii, ¶ 39.   ³ Ibid., ch. iii, ¶ 2.
    ⁴ Ibid., ch. iii, ¶ 4.   ⁵ Ibid., ch. iii, ¶ 10.

but he does so only for the benefit of people who, unlike himself, cannot see that such individuality justifies itself. He ends the chapter with a complaint. 'The greatness of England,' he says, 'is now all collective; individually small, we only appear capable of anything great by our habit of combining . . .'[1]

The last two chapters of the essay discuss the proper limits to the authority of society over the individual. It has often been objected against Mill, that his criterion is difficult to apply and does not leave much liberty to the individual. As he himself admits, since no one is completely isolated, almost any action is liable to harm or to benefit other people. A man can do nothing seriously harmful to himself, without injury to at least some other persons, whose welfare depends upon his being able to act in ways in which the harm he does himself prevents him from acting. But Mill is not much impressed by the admissions he has to make. It may well be true that we cannot say of any class of actions that they never injure other people, and that we cannot, therefore, say that people ought never to be prevented from doing them. But this in no way invalidates Mill's criterion, nor does it make it less easy to apply than any other. Few moral theories assert that actions of any given type are always right or always wrong; and Mill has as much right to be vague as any other moralist in a matter in which greater precision is not possible. As for the objection that Mill's criterion leaves almost no liberty to the individual, it is not well founded; for though any kind of action may sometimes injure other people nearly as much as or more than it injures the agent, it does not follow that the actions which injure them not at all, or so little as not to be worth regarding, are few. Indeed, we all know they are many, and that people love to interfere with what does not concern them. We may argue, then, that Mill's criterion is not strictly consistent with his utilitarian principles, but we cannot say that it is impossible to apply it or unimportant to do so.

Mill is, indeed, quite aware that the strict application of his criterion must deprive many people of powers they now possess, for it must curtail the authority of husbands over wives and of parents over children. Mill also explains that the case for laissez-faire in the economic sphere has nothing to do with his defence of individual liberty. His criterion does not exclude the most extreme

[1] Ibid., ch. iii, ¶ 16.

socialism, though it does, of course, exclude the sort of totalitarian government with which we are familiar to-day. At the end of his essay, Mill gives us three rules for the limitation of state interference, even in those spheres in which men's actions clearly affect other people as much as themselves—that is to say, in those spheres in which his liberal criterion does not exclude interference. No government should, he thinks, interfere with its subjects' actions, though they affect other people as much as themselves, whenever one or more of three conditions hold good: when the action is likely to be better done by private persons than by the government; when, though private persons usually do it less well than the officers of government, it is still desirable that they should do it as a means to their own education; and whenever there is a danger of adding unnecessarily to the government's power. By this last condition, Mill probably means to warn us against granting to governments powers, which they may need for useful purposes not otherwise to be achieved, but which will enable them to grow so strong that they can abuse their powers with impunity. Mill also warns us against the dangers of a powerful bureaucracy. These must, he thinks, always be great, however benevolent the bureaucrats. 'For the governors,' he says, 'are as much slaves of their organisation and discipline as the governed are of the governors.'[1] These are Mill's arguments in favour of private enterprise. He puts them shortly at the end of his essay, and it is a pity that he found no time to develop them. By temperament and by experience he was admirably suited to make the fine distinctions on which the reconciliation of liberty and efficient government must always depend.

When Mill wrote his essay on *Liberty*, democrats were ardent believers in democracy. They were full of confidence in themselves and in their final victory. Mill's essay is therefore a warning to enthusiasts. It assumes that democracy will come and that when it comes it will be strong. It is a plea to the powerful not to abuse their powers. It is addressed, as a work written in English must be, principally to the English-speaking peoples, a group of nations exceptionally vigorous, self-confident and politically experienced. It is precisely among them that democracy is to-day most firmly established, and it is to them that an essay, which warns men of the dangers *from* and not *to* democracy, is still the most useful. The

[1] Ibid., ch. v, ¶ 21.

English-speaking peoples do not now praise democracy as they did when it was a novelty, but they are not tempted to abandon it. Its ways are their ways, much more so to-day than when Mill was alive. If democracy is in danger among them, it is not so much from internal collapse as from foreign war. Mill's warnings still apply in a large part of the world inhabited by the richest and the strongest nations.

We are all busy, nowadays, describing the evils of bureaucracy, remembering, no doubt, how well we managed our lives before governments took so many of our cares upon them. We tell each other daily that we are not sufficiently alive to dangers about which we never stop talking. Perhaps it was because he knew his own people that Mill was content to say so little about bureaucracy. But his warnings against the tyranny of opinion are always necessary, though it may be that Englishmen and Americans need them less to-day than their ancestors did a hundred years ago. Mill was thinking of the respectable middle class to which he himself belonged, and of the America described by de Tocqueville and still dominated by rural Puritanism. The less censorious and better-humoured working classes have now a greater influence in this country, while both here and in America the towns, always more tolerant of novelty, set the fashions for the villages. The present danger in this country is not so much that those who have unpopular and valuable opinions will be ill-treated as that no one will take any notice of them. From the enormous variety of opinions, experiences and tastes collected for our benefit in free and easily accessible libraries, museums and galleries, we take refuge in the narrow circles of our intellectual friends, among whom a few familiar ideas and prejudices circulate.

In his essay on *Representative Government*, Mill again gives expression to his distrust of democracy. But he thinks that, whatever its defects, it is still the best form of government. He admits that it is unsuited to many peoples, since it requires greater abilities and greater self-control from all the members of the community than does any other form of government. It is only, he thinks, at a comparatively late stage in their development that a people become capable of representative government. But once they are capable of it, it is not only more suited to them than any other kind, it also makes them better men than they used to be. Mill returns again to the idea of self-improvement for its own sake, an idea that never fails to attract him though it is the negation of the utilitarian principles he professes. He thinks it the great merit of representative democracy, not that it makes men happier (though he believes it does so) but that it makes them more intelligent, more virtuous and more responsible than they would be without it. 'One of the benefits of freedom is,' he says, 'that under it the ruler cannot pass by the people's minds, and mend their affairs for them without amending them.'[1] 'Evil for evil,' he thinks, 'a good despotism in a country at all advanced in civilization, is more noxious than a bad one; for it is more relaxing and enervating to the thoughts, feelings and energies of the people.'[2]

Here again, because of what we know has happened since Mill's death, we must qualify his opinions. He had not our means of knowing how bad a bad despotism can be. Though it may not relax men's minds, it corrupts and debases them. It puts fear and reckless enthusiasm in the place of all the social affections that hold a community together; and when that fear and enthusiasm are gone, there is nothing left. In their secret hearts, men are ashamed of being treated like dumb animals, to be praised, threatened or whipped whenever it suits their masters. When this shame is intolerable and they dare not protest, they are diminished in their own eyes and the injury done to them is the greatest that governments can do to men. An evil despotism destroys man's self-respect as a good one can never do. But when Mill talked of a bad despotism, he had nothing worse in mind than some of the small German and Italian states and Imperial Russia. They were bad enough, but their power to compel and to humiliate was small indeed compared with what more recent governments have possessed.

Though Mill praises representative government because it educates the governed, he does not ignore the arguments which had appeared convincing to his father and to Bentham. He also believes that the rights and interests of every man are, in most cases, best defended by himself, and that therefore every man ought to have some influence with the government on whose actions his welfare largely depends. The more free and active each citizen, the more prosperous the state. The radical utilitarian doctrine, that freedom is the means to prosperity, and prosperity the means to

---

[1] *Representative Government,* ch. iii, ¶ 6.   [2] Ibid., ch. iii, ¶ 7.

happiness, is never neglected by the younger Mill. But it is only one half of his argument for representative democracy.

Representative Government is a much longer essay than *Liberty*, and it is full of good arguments. But to the political philosopher it is the less interesting of the two. It raises fewer theoretical problems, and, with the exception of a few chapters, it is a treatise on political institutions. *Liberty* is incomparably the best and the most eloquent of all Mill's works. Among modern writers, only Machiavelli, Hobbes and Rousseau have dealt with a political subject in a way that makes a more powerful and immediate impression on the reader's mind.

3. *Utilitarianism*

Mill wrote this essay to defend his father and Bentham from the attacks made upon them. His defence is not a good one. He was too much impressed by the attack to know how to meet it. With so many concessions made to the enemy, what should have been a defence reads like an apology. Mill was in the difficult position of a man whose loyalty is stronger than his faith, who cannot be blind and yet dare not see too much. Such people do not construct the most impressive philosophical systems, nor do they strike the hardest blows, but when they have the intelligence and honesty of Mill, their predicament is always instructive.

Mill begins his essay by distinguishing between what he calls the 'intuitionist' and 'inductive' schools of morals. His own opinion, he says, is that questions of ultimate ends are not amenable to direct proof. Whatever can be proved to be good, must be so by being shown to be a means to something admitted to be good without proof. He then goes on to say that he has no intention of adopting the view of the intuitionists, that the principles of morals are self-evident. Though direct proof is impossible, 'considerations may be presented capable of determining the intellect either to give or to withhold its assent to the doctrine; and this is equivalent to proof'.[1]

What exactly does Mill mean? If he believes, as he appears to do, that the greatest happiness principle is not self-evident, he has, as a philosopher, no alternative except to offer his readers evidence

[1] *Utilitarianism*, ch. 1, ¶ 5.

of its truth. And this is, in fact, precisely what he does try to do. The whole of his essay is devoted to the task; and therefore all its arguments rest upon the assumption that questions of ultimate ends are amenable to proof. Hume certainly thought they were; and there is nothing incompatible with this belief in his dictum that 'Reason is and ought to be the slave of the passions'. But Mill is guilty of a confusion. If you say that an end is ultimate, you merely say it is desired for its own sake and not as a means to something else. But the question of whether or not it is so desired is as much amenable to disproof or proof as any other matter of fact. All that Hume meant by his dictum, is that reason cannot tell us what we ought to desire for its own sake. But if we wish to discover what men do so desire, we must observe their behaviour; and if any one denies our conclusions, we must then point to the evidence. Though reason does not prescribe ultimate ends, it enables us to discover what they are. Whoever accepts the view that morals is an experimental science must believe at least two things: that the statement that men ought to desire something for its own sake is, when fully analysed, merely a statement about their desires and feelings; and that questions of ultimate ends are therefore always amenable to proof. Hume does sometimes use language that suggests he does not hold the second of these beliefs, but this is only his careless manner of expressing himself. He is, in fact, quite aware of what is implied by his attempt to introduce the experimental method into morals. But John Stuart Mill, making a similar attempt, is not so well aware of what he is doing. Hence his curious statement that something cannot be proved, though considerations equivalent to proof can be brought to induce men to accept it.

Mill admits that some pleasures are higher than others. He tells us that if one of two pleasures is, 'by those who are completely acquainted with both, placed so far above the other that they prefer it, even though knowing it to be attended with a greater amount of discontent, and would not resign it for any quantity of the other pleasure which their nature is capable of, we are justified in ascribing to the preferred enjoyment a superiority in quality, so far outweighing quantity, as to render it, in comparison, of small account'.[1] Mill's words suggest that the superiority is in the thing preferred and does not merely consist in its being preferred.

[1] Ibid., ch. ii, ¶ 5.

An argument very like Mill's is used by Socrates in the ninth book of the *Republic*. He there distinguishes between three classes of men: lovers of wisdom, lovers of honour, and lovers of gain. Each class, when asked which sort of life is the pleasantest, will praise their own and prefer it to the others. How, then, is the question to be decided between them? What criterion can be used in such a case? No other, according to Socrates, than experience. The lover of wisdom has, he thinks, the greatest experience of all the pleasures that are in question. He has tasted them all, while the lovers of honour and of gain know nothing of the pleasures to be derived from the pursuit of knowledge. He has taken the measure of their lives, while they know nothing of his. He alone is competent to judge; and his verdict is final.

Such an argument may convince when we are trying to discover which of three engines is best suited to our purpose. It is an argument we can use, when we have no better one, to help us choose the most efficient of several alternative means to the same end. But used as Socrates and Mill use it, it carries no conviction at all. No man has ever known the pleasures experienced by another; he can only say that, among his own, he prefers some to the rest. If Socrates preferred philosophy to sensuality and praise, it was because he was the sort of man that nature made him. His love of wisdom and his passion for exposing pretentious ignorance caused him to attach the highest value to pleasures that to other men may appear insipid. We most of us derive our greatest happiness from doing what we can do best. But there are men who can rise superior to the prejudices created by pride in their own talents. Montaigne was as full of curiosity as any man and as convinced as Socrates of his own ignorance, but he did not therefore suppose that his favourite pleasures were the supreme good. He even thought it unworthy of a man of honour that he should be at pains to get the better of an argument.

To justify his preference for the verdict of 'those most competent to judge', Mill says that comparisons between qualities of pleasure are not different in principle from comparisons between quantities. He says 'there is no other tribunal to be referred to even on the question of quantity. What means are there of determining which is the acutest of two pains, or the intensest of two pleasurable sensations, except the general suffrage of those who are familiar with both? Neither pains nor pleasures are homogeneous, and pain is always heterogeneous with pleasure.'[1] This argument does not establish the point that Mill wishes to make. The fact that people prefer some pleasures to others is no evidence that those they prefer are either superior in quality or greater than the others, unless it is first assumed that people normally prefer what is superior or greater to what is inferior or less. But though the argument does not serve Mill's purpose, it does what he never intended; for it cuts away the foundations of the Benthamite felicific calculus. If pleasures and pains are not homogeneous, then the calculation and comparison of their quantities is in principle impossible; all that we can calculate is the frequency and order of men's preferences. So that, already by the tenth page of an essay written in its defence, Mill has made two wide breaches in his father's and Bentham's system. He has asserted that some pleasures are qualitatively superior to others, and he has implied that the felicific calculus is impossible.

It has been said that, when Mill admits that some pleasures are higher than others, he is untrue to his own doctrine that nothing is good but pleasure. For if one pleasure is higher than another, that in respect of which it is higher is not pleasure but some other thing, which must therefore be admitted to be good. This simple argument is, perhaps, not as conclusive as it looks. If a man were to say that nothing is beautiful except colour and then to place the colours in an order of beauty, it would not follow that he was admitting that anything but colour could be beautiful. The difference between one colour and another is not a difference of degree, nor yet is it a difference in respect of anything except colour. So, too, the higher and the lower pleasures, though different in kind, may yet differ only in respect of pleasure. If this were so, it might then be true both that nothing is good but pleasure and that some kinds of pleasure are superior to others, though neither more intense nor of longer duration. There is, perhaps, no reason for supposing any such thing; but if Mill chooses to take up this position, better arguments than those used hitherto must be found to dislodge him from it.

Mill's theory of pleasure is his theory about the ultimate end of human action. This end is, he thinks, a life 'exempt as far as

[1] Ibid., ch. ii, ¶ 8.

K

possible from pain, and as rich as possible in enjoyments, both in point of quantity and quality.' It is also the standard of morality, for morality consists of those rules of conduct whose general observance will secure, as far as possible, this sort of life to all mankind. 'In the golden rule of Jesus of Nazareth,' says Mill, 'we read the complete spirit of the ethics of utility. To do as you would be done by, and to love your neighbour as yourself, constitute the ideal perfection of utilitarian morality.'[1] This is not the sort of language that would come naturally to the lips of Bentham or James Mill. But it is typical of their greatest disciple. *Do as you would be done by* is a prudential maxim, whose ablest English exponent is Thomas Hobbes. *Love your neighbour as yourself* is a rule of a quite different order, though its observance may have much the same visible effects. No one better than the younger Mill could feel the essential difference between the two rules. If he puts them together, it is to lend nobility to the utilitarian doctrine, and not to prove that Christianity is sensible.

Having explained the nature of the good life, Mill then goes on to define moral obligation. It is, he says, the internal sanction of duty, and he carefully distinguishes it from the external sanction, which is no more than the hope of favour and the fear of displeasure from our fellow-men or from God. The internal sanction of duty is, he says, 'a feeling of our own mind, a pain more or less intense, attendant on violation of duty'.[2] Now this feeling is 'all encrusted over with collateral associations, derived from sympathy, from love, and still more from fear; from all the forms of religious feeling, from the recollections of childhood and of all our past life; from self-esteem, desire of the esteem of others, and occasionally even self-abasement'.[3] It is this extreme complexity, according to Mill, that leads men to attribute a mystical character to moral obligation, whose binding force consists in 'a mass of feeling which must be broken through in order to do what violates our standard of right'.[4]

What Mill is describing is not the rightness of an action, but the peculiar emotion men often feel when they are considering how they should act. The right action, for the younger Mill as for his father and Bentham, is the one which the prospective agent believes will lead to the happiest consequences. It is not in his account

---

[1] Ibid., ch. ii, ¶ 18.   [2] Ibid., ch. iii, ¶ 4.   [3] Ibid., ch. iii, ¶ 4.
[4] Ibid., ch. iii, ¶ 4.

of right action but of the feeling of moral obligation that Mill parts company with his father and Bentham. The external sanctions of duty, to which both the elder utilitarians devote so much attention, are described in a few words, and it is on the internal sanction that the younger Mill lavishes his descriptive powers. He says not one word to suggest that the feeling of moral obligation is merely the indissoluble product of past associations of men's selfish desires and expectations. Sympathy, love and the religious emotions, as well as fear, memory and self-esteem, are the joint creators of this rich and powerful emotion, to which men have attributed a mystical character. So different is his emotional experience from his father's that he even finds room in his analysis for self-abasement. Whatever the true account of the matter, his description is certainly more plausible than either Bentham's or the elder Mill's. More seriously even than its author, he took Hume's excellent advice, that in moral philosophy over-simplification is the great danger. It is when, without knowing it, he moves furthest from Bentham and his father, without feeling the need to excuse either himself or them, that the younger Mill is at his best.

So far, so good. But Mill still has to explain how it is that we come to feel morally obliged to behave in accordance with the greatest happiness principle. He admits that the conscience can be educated in almost any direction. There is almost nothing that we cannot be taught to be ashamed of or to feel morally obliged to do. But he thinks that there is nevertheless a natural tendency in the human mind to associate the feeling of moral obligation with actions that normally produce the greatest happiness. Associations of it with other principles are wholly of 'artificial' creation, and they yield, by degrees, to the dissolving force of intellectual analysis. On the other hand, there is a 'powerful natural sentiment' which reinforces the attachment of the feeling of moral obligation with the utilitarian principle. This powerful sentiment is the desire to be 'in unity' with our fellow-creatures; in other words, it is the social instinct. Mill, however, does not explain how it is that the social instinct attaches the feeling of moral obligation to the utilitarian principle. He just assumes that it must be so, that the point is too obvious to be worth discussing. But it appears obvious only to those who accept the utilitarian philosophy. Mere observers of human behaviour are not so easily convinced. There are, for instance, many sociologists who would agree that the social instinct, whatever it is, attaches the moral sentiments to certain rules of conduct 'useful' to the society in question; but there are few of them who would define 'useful' as 'conducive to the greatest happiness'.

So far, except for some ambiguities and a few plausible arguments of his own, the younger Mill's moral system is closer to Hume's than to his father's and Bentham's. The one concession he has made to the Benthamite form of utilitarianism is his statement 'that actions are right in proportion as they tend to promote happiness, wrong as they tend to produce the reverse of happiness'.[1] But in the fourth chapter of the essay, he abandons Hume and produces arguments whose weakness would have been noticed by no one more quickly than by the great Scottish philosopher. Mill wishes to prove that happiness is desirable, and he says: 'The only proof capable of being given that an object is visible, is that people actually see it ... In like manner, I apprehend, the sole evidence it is possible to produce that anything is desirable is that people actually do desire it ... No reason can be given why the general happiness is desirable, except that each person, so far as he believes it to be attainable, desires his own happiness. This, however, being a fact, we have not only all the proof which the case admits of, but all which it is possible to require, that happiness is good: that each person's happiness is a good to that person, and the general happiness, therefore, a good to the aggregate of all persons.'[2]

The passage just quoted has often been attacked. Nobody but Mill ever supposed that *desirable* stands to *desired* as *visible* to *seen*. Visible means 'capable of being seen' and desirable 'worthy of being desired', so that while a thing's being seen proves it is visible, its being desired is no evidence that it is desirable. And it is equally clear that there is no argument from each person's happiness being his good to the general happiness as the good of all.

Mill's next object is to prove that nothing but happiness is desirable. He begins by admitting that many things besides happiness are in fact desired. Why, then, are they not desirable? Is it because they are no more than means to happiness, which alone is desired for its own sake? No such simple solution will satisfy Mill. 'Utilitarian moralists', he tells us, ' ... not only place virtue at the very head of the things which are good as means to the ultimate

---

[1] Ibid., ch. ii, ¶ 2.   [2] Ibid., ch. iv, ¶ 3.

end, but they also recognize as a psychological fact the possibility of its being, to the individual, a good in itself, without looking to any end beyond it; and hold that the mind is not in a right state, not in a state conformable to Utility, not in the state most conducive to the general happiness, unless it does love virtue in this manner . . '[1] Once virtue is loved in this way, it becomes a part of man's happiness. How this can be is explained by Mill a few pages later on, when he says: 'I believe that . . . desiring a thing and finding it pleasant, aversion to it and thinking of it as painful, are phenomena entirely inseparable, or rather two aspects of the same phenomenon; in strictness of language, two different modes of naming the same fact; that to think of a thing as desirable (unless for the sake of its consequences), and to think of it as pleasant, are one and the same thing; and that to desire anything, except in proportion as the idea of it is pleasant, is a physical and metaphysical impossibility.'[2] The gist of this argument seems to be: nothing is desired for its own sake except happiness. Some things, like virtue, which were originally desired because they are a means to happiness, are now often desired for their own sake. But to desire a thing for its own sake is to find it pleasant. Therefore virtue, once merely a means to happiness, is now also a constituent of it; and it is a means all the more efficient because it is also a part of the end. This argument depends upon a simple confusion to which both Butler and Hume had pointed in their refutations of Hobbesian egoism. It may be true that, whenever we desire something, we take pleasure at the thought of obtaining it; but we have this pleasure before we obtain what we desire. This pleasure is, strictly speaking, the companion and not the object of desire. But apart from this pleasure, there need be no other in question. To take pleasure at the thought of being virtuous is not the same thing as to desire virtue because it is pleasant. Mill, failing to make this distinction, found it possible to assert that to desire something is to think of it as pleasant. This assertion is false; but even if it were true, Mill's argument would be none the better. For, if to desire something is to find it pleasant, to desire virtue is still not to desire pleasure. To desire virtue is, then, to find virtue pleasant, but to desire pleasure is to find pleasure (and not virtue) pleasant, so that virtue is no nearer to becoming

[1] Ibid., ch. iv, ¶ 5.   [2] Ibid., ch. iv, ¶ 10.

a constituent of happiness. No juggling with words and no false psychology can effect a reconciliation in such a case.

In the last and fifth chapter of the essay, Mill discusses the connexion between justice and morality. This chapter is, perhaps, the best of the five. Taking etymology for his guide, Mill supposes that the primitive notion of justice (for instance, among the Jews of the Old Testament) was simply conformity to law. The distinction between morality and legality, the notion of an 'unjust law', belongs to a more developed society. It is only to be found among the Greeks and the Romans at a fairly advanced stage in their development. But though the distinction between law and morality is nowadays clear, the connexion between the two is still close. 'It is a part of the notion of Duty in every one of its forms,' says Mill, 'that a person may rightly be compelled to fulfil it. Duty is a thing which may be exacted from a person, as one exacts a debt.'[1]

Mill distinguishes between justice, in the narrow sense, which is merely doing what the law enjoins, and justice, in the larger sense, which is doing all one's duties to assignable persons, that is, to all persons who have a right to expect us to act in any particular way. He also talks of general duties that imply no rights in assignable persons. He offers as an example our duty to be charitable though no person may have a right to assistance from us. These general duties fall outside the sphere of justice, for the 'two essential ingredients in the sentiment of justice are', says Mill, 'the desire to punish a person who has done harm, and the knowledge or belief that there is some definite individual or individuals to whom harm has been done.'[2] 'The sentiment of justice . . . is . . . the natural feeling of retaliation or vengeance, rendered by intellect and sympathy applicable to those injuries . . . which wound us through, or in common with, society at large. This sentiment, in itself, has nothing moral in it; what is moral is the exclusive subordination of it to the social sympathies . . . For the natural feeling would make us resent indiscriminately whatever anyone does that is disagreeable to us; but when moralised by the social feeling, it only acts in the directions conformable to the general good.'[3]

There is a certain resemblance between Hume's account of the psychological origins of justice and this theory of Mill's. But Mill's real debt is not to Hume but to Alexander Bain, to his book

[1] Ibid., ch. v, ¶ 14.   [2] Ibid., ch. v, ¶ 17.   [3] Ibid., ch. v, ¶ 21.

on the *Mind* and to the chapter in it entitled 'The Ethical Emotions or the Moral Sense'. Although Mill, like Hume, assigns an important role to sympathy, he does so at an earlier stage in the process. Hume had said that no emotion is strong enough to control man's self-love and to make him just. If self-love is to be controlled, it must turn upon itself and set limits to its own action. This it does, whenever a man takes a little thought and understands that his strongest passion is better satisfied by its restraint than its liberty. Self-love is the original motive that brought justice into existence, and sympathy is needed only to explain how it became a virtue. It is sympathy with the public interest that makes us approve the practice of justice, and it is this approval that makes it a virtue.

Mill's account puts a much greater burden on sympathy. Justice, for him, is not an unnatural thing, begotten by reflexion out of self-love, and later crowned a virtue by sympathy. Justice owes to sympathy its existence and not only its moral dignity. It is the natural feeling of vengeance applied, not by intellect alone but by sympathy as well, to the injuries done to any man. It is in this way that Mill associates our selfish and our unselfish feelings in the generation of justice, for what intellect does, among other things, is to teach us that by defending others we defend ourselves. Justice is the product of two sentiments, each as natural as the other: the instinct of self-preservation and the feeling of sympathy. The part of intellect, which is Mill's name for what Hume calls reflexion, is, we must suppose, to enlighten both these sentiments. Mill, even at his best, is not free from ambiguity, but if this is his meaning, he is probably nearer the truth than is Hume.

Mill's final purpose is to explain the difference between our emotional reactions to the unjust and the inexpedient; for, on strict utilitarian premises, the former can be only a special case of the latter. He says that certain kinds of conduct are much more generally useful than others. They form, as he puts it, the 'very groundwork' of our existence in society. Our desire to safeguard this groundwork gathers around it feelings so much more intense than those to which we are liable on less important occasions, that 'the difference of degree . . . becomes a real difference in kind'.[1] Hence the need we feel to make an absolute distinction between what is

---

[1] Ibid., ch. v, ¶ 25.

right or wrong, on the one hand, and what is expedient or inexpedient, on the other.

There is not much left of Benthamite utilitarianism when John
Stuart Mill has completed his defence of it. What is left is, strictly
speaking, not utilitarianism at all, but a kind of naturalistic ethics
that it would be misleading to call a variety of hedonism. Yet in
Mill's strange concoction there still are to be found remnants of
the parental creed, floating on the surface, separate from one
another, solid and insoluble. But for all its faults, Mill's essay, in
which he continually turns away from what he professes to describe,
is still worth the closest study; not only because it enables the
student to exercise the destructive faculties indispensable to the
philosopher, but also because it contains much that is plausible and
suggestive. There is little to be gained by unravelling the tangled
threads of Bentham's fundamental arguments. With Mill it is
different; the study of his confusions and errors is nearly always
profitable.

CHAPTER IX

THE UTILITARIANS

THE utilitarian doctrine, established by Hume on foundations laid by Hobbes, is the greatest English contribution to moral and political philosophy. If it is no longer thought adequate as an explanation of men's moral and political behaviour, this is certainly not because any other philosophy has taken its place. Utilitarianism is destroyed and no part of it left standing. But it has not had a successor. There is to-day in England no one system that enjoys anything like the predominance once enjoyed in intellectual circles[1] by utilitarianism. A number of theories, mostly of continental origin, are cherished by small groups of Englishmen, but none of them deserves to be called predominant. We are all democrats, perhaps, and it may be that we are also, in some senses of that word, all socialists. But democracy and socialism, as they are talked of in contemporary England, are not political and moral philosophies; the principles from which they can be (and are) derived are too many and too different from one another. We have to-day no distinguishable group of English philosophers, all preaching more or less the same doctrine and providing the intellectuals with most of their commonplaces when they discuss morals and politics. But the utilitarians were once in England what the Marxists were for a few decades in Germany, the social and political thinkers whose ideas had the widest currency though they were also the most vigorously attacked. The utilitarians were the doctrinaires of England, no less native to the country of their origin than the German Marxists.

I have already, in discussing the theories of the more important utilitarians, criticized the assumptions on which they rest. Hedonism in general, and utilitarianism as an instance of it, are doctrines that have been often attacked. Most of the traditional arguments, as well as others discovered by himself, have been clearly

---

[1] I believe that, in using this phrase, I deceive no one. By that time there were already intellectuals in the world. Clever men had already discovered that the difference between themselves and the rest of mankind was much greater than Galileo, Descartes and Newton supposed.

145

stated by Professor Moore in his book *Principia Ethica*. Not all
Professor Moore's arguments are equally convincing, the effective-
ness of several depending upon the assumption that his interpretation of the doctrine he is attacking is the correct one. For instance,
he proves that egoism, a doctrine to which not only Hobbes but
also several of the utilitarians adhered, is self-contradictory. Yet
it is self-contradictory only if goodness is some such quality as
Professor Moore thinks it is. In that case, it is absurd to say that
anything is good for only one man and not for all other men as
well. If Professor Moore's account of goodness is the true one,
nothing can be good for any particular man any more than it can
be round or red only for him. And this, of course, must be so,
even if the good thing in question should be the state of his own
mind. But if good is defined as Hobbes defined it, as whatever is
the object of desire, there obviously can be private goods, in the
only sense required to save Hobbes's theory from self-contradiction.
Again, in his argument against John Stuart Mill's assertion that,
though only pleasure is good, some pleasures are superior to others,
Professor Moore says: 'If you say, as Mill does, that the quality of
pleasure is to be taken into account, then you are no longer holding
that pleasure *alone* is good as an end, since you imply that something
else, something which is *not* in all pleasures, is also good as an end.'[1]
He illustrates the point he wishes to make by substituting the notion
of colour for pleasure. If we suppose that colour alone is good, we
can, according to Professor Moore, have no reason for preferring
one colour to another. But this is true only if we suppose that it is
abstract colour alone that is good. There is, however, no reason
for believing that the natural interpretation of the statement,
'colour alone is good', is the one put upon it by Professor Moore.
It might more naturally be taken to mean that there is nothing good
about anything except its colour; and this interpretation does not
exclude the possibility that some colours should be better than others.
This is true whatever *good* may mean, provided only that it does not
mean *pleasant*. Now, since Mill defined goodness in terms of desire
and said that to desire a thing is to find it pleasant, it is clear that he
did consider goodness the same thing as pleasure. But that is not
the point Professor Moore makes against him. He argues that,
whatever good may mean, to say that only colour is good is to

[1] *Principia Ethica*, p. 80.

imply that no colour can be better than another. If it can be proved that Mill, already committed to definite views about both goodness and pleasure, ought not to have said that one sort of pleasure is better than another, the proof must be different from Professor Moore's. For his proof implies what is false: that the statements 'only pleasure is good' and 'some pleasures are better than others' are incompatible. But though Professor Moore places to his own credit some unnecessary dialectical victories, most of the arguments in *Principia Ethica* are, I think, convincing. And if that is so, then utilitarianism, however qualified to make it look more plausible, is an untenable theory.

The utilitarians have been called rationalists, even by the people who have most successfully pulled their arguments to pieces. The compliment is deserved, and the collapse of their system does not seriously detract from its value. What reason has set up, reason can best destroy. Everyone who seeks to convince by argument has a common ground with the utilitarians. But everyone who seeks to convince by argument also necessarily exposes a large surface to hostile attack. He tries to make his meaning clear; and because clarity is more easily attained than truth, he must expect to be the sooner corrected the more readily he is understood. The utilitarians were more listened to than revered. This did at least mean that their reputations never stood in the way of truth. In more recent times, in political and moral philosophy, more particularly since Hegel and Marx, the rule has been: tout comprendre, c'est ne rien pardonner.

It is interesting that the utilitarians, the most English of all schools of political and moral philosophers, should have been such unrelenting rationalists, deriving so much from so few and such simple assumptions. For the defect of which the English are most proud is that they are not logical. They say they do not like consistency, or even the appearance of it, when it is only to be had at the expense of truth. And this, as experience teaches us, is the price usually paid for it. Better a muddle that touches reality at many points than a coherent system which, if it touches it at some, must, owing to its rigidity, miss it at all the others. Better a variety of practical rules, none of them too clearly expressed and not necessarily compatible with one another, than an apparently well-constructed doctrine which has, among other disadvantages, this one, that it makes it easier for other people to prove that we have not lived up to our own principles. The Anglo-Saxon ideal is supposed to be something like the philosophy of the American Supreme Court, which has at its disposal any number of unrelated precedents enabling it to interpret a reticent constitution in whatever way it thinks best. But in moral and political philosophy, the English have had as steady a preference for logic and simplicity as any other European people. Indeed, if the student of politics and morals wishes to escape for a little from implacable logic and the most self-confident simplicity, he must turn away from the English, whether utilitarians or contractualists, and seek refuge in the more muddled, emotional and extravagant writings of Frenchmen and Germans. It is from Rousseau, Kant, Saint-Simon and Marx, seldom lucid and sometimes mere purveyors of nonsense,[1] that he can learn many things that are true, though badly expressed, and that escaped the notice of the high-and-dry intellectual utilitarians.

Though his own views may fail to convince, Kant has shown that the simple psychology of the eighteenth-century moralists does not explain the facts. The desire for pleasure, prudence and egoism, even if sympathy is added to them, are not the stuff of which to make a plausible theory of morals. Whatever men may be doing when they are acting morally, they are not seeking pleasure, nor are they being selfish, prudent or sympathetic. Morality curbs egoism, is often indifferent to pleasure and usually overrides prudence. These are the undeniable facts vouched for by our daily experience. That society could not hold together without morality is also a fact, but it does not follow that morality is a kind of social insurance, in which each individual finds his account. To treat the moral laws prevailing in any society as if their function must be to create a harmony between otherwise divergent interests, is a serious fault of method. It implies an assumption that the true answer to the problem investigated by the moral philosopher must be of a certain kind, but the utilitarians had no good reason for making this assumption. Many of them made no serious attempt to answer the questions they pretended to ask, such as: what is morality? and, what is the State? They did not analyse the moral

---

[1] I use this word in the technical and inoffensive sense habitual among philosophers. There is, of course, nonsense and nonsense, some of it a credit to the heart and even the head of its author. Though the truth should lie far removed from both their systems, there will always be a world of difference between Kant and Hegel.

behaviour of men in the attempt to discover what it is they are doing when they behave morally. Nor did they study their political behaviour or the institutions maintained by and determining that behaviour. What they did was to attempt answers to quite other questions, of which the most important was: under what circumstances will each man's efforts to be as happy as possible promote the greatest happiness of all men? They did not distinguish, as they ought to have done, between the analysis of social phenomena and the solution of practical problems; and they were too much inclined to believe that to attempt the latter was to achieve the former. The utilitarians who came closest to making a genuine attempt to answer, not only questions about how what they thought desirable could be achieved, but also others that belong more properly to moral and political philosophy were Hume and John Stuart Mill. They did not, like Bentham, confuse the analysis of moral and political behaviour with the solution of practical problems. But in their case, too, the careless attempt to find compatible answers to quite dissimilar questions led to false assumptions or to serious distortions of truth.

In the sphere of ethics, Hume took notice of two questions: what are the characteristics of moral and immoral actions? and, what is the function of morality? He gave a separate answer to each, understanding what Bentham and James Mill never seem to have done, that one would not do for both. His answer to the first was his description of the moral sentiments and their operation; his answer to the second, the bare statement that these sentiments are so directed that they induce men to do what will increase happiness, and abstain from what will diminish it. But for the truth of this statement, the greatest of experimental philosophers never troubled to produce one shred of evidence. So little was he aware of the difficulty confronting him, that he thought it enough to appeal to the common sense of mankind. The younger Mill, when it suited him, also made assumptions equally convenient and unsupported. He did not like that men should interfere with each other except to prevent harm to others. Yet, though he was a utilitarian, he never troubled to show that this non-interference would promote happiness. He also believed in 'self-realization'. But he never explained to his readers how he conceived this 'self-realization'. Did he mean by it whatever a man would become if other men interfered with him as little as possible? This is the only meaning of the word which makes it obvious that liberty, as Mill defined it, is the condition of 'self-realization'. If, for instance, 'self-realization' is taken to mean 'as good or valuable a life as the individual is capable of living', it is no longer obvious that the liberty described by Mill is what makes it possible. Plato also believed in 'self-realization', and in the *Laws* he advocated a secret police. And what is the connexion between 'self-realization' and 'happiness'? Mill did not even ask this question. He did not do what, as a utilitarian, he should have done. However subtle or shrewd a philosopher may otherwise be, there is always a simplicity that shapes his thoughts and prevents him from asking questions inconvenient to his own theories.

The utilitarians, even those who most often claimed to be experimental philosophers, were all dogmatists. They supposed, when they gave the matter a thought, that the principles from which they started were generalizations from experience. But in fact they were nothing of the kind. The truth is that only one of them, Hume, knew what was implied by the claim to have introduced the 'experimental method' into morals. He described the method well enough, but, as we have seen, he never used it. As he was a man of the world and an historian, his assumptions were more plausible than those of Bentham and the elder Mill. But they were not seriously tested. What could better show how little Hume understood the difficulties of his task than his belief that one man could accomplish it? He never thought it necessary to warn his readers that his own theory was the product of one man's experience, and that no one had yet made a real study of the facts that theory was supposed to explain. His assumptions are of the kind that intelligent and experienced men might think plausible as they discussed them of an evening over their port. They sound sensible, but there is no real evidence that they are true.

In the political field, the great error of the utilitarians was their individualism. By this I do not mean their belief that nothing is desirable except the happiness of individuals. For that is a judgment of value as much entitled to respect as any other. I mean only their assumption that the general structure of society can be adequately explained in terms of men's desires and purposes. Society, government and morality are not means to individual ends; they are not contrivances made by men to suit their purposes. They are the effects of human actions done with a view to other effects. Had not men behaved as they did, these things never would have come into existence, but they were not the ends of the actions that produced them. It is only very recently that we have come to understand even a little about the societies in which we live. The social and political institutions that surround us were not made by us, nor is it true that they continue to exist because we understand and find them good. Society is not made by men, though social laws are nothing but laws of human behaviour. Because it is true that society is nothing except men and their habits and laws, and that all social institutions are the products of human activities, it does not follow that men make societies. For to make is to contrive for a purpose, and implies a conscious end and a knowledge of means. It is only because we use words that suggest purposes to describe nearly all the consequences of human activities that it comes natural to us to describe social and political institutions as if they were made by men. We do, of course, have our theories about these institutions and we have our purposes; and so also did our ancestors. However ignorant the theories and foolish the purposes, they determine human behaviour and so affect social institutions. Men are always trying to adapt their institutions to their desires, and to some extent they succeed. But all this makes it no less true that these institutions are not the realizations of human purposes, and that they affect these purposes just as much (and perhaps much more) than they are affected by them.

The utilitarians, above all men, were determined not to be the dupes of words, and they destroyed more nonsense than any other modern school of philosophers. With occasional lapses, they wrote with unusual lucidity. Yet it may be that language got the better of them just when it was most necessary that they should be its masters. The political vocabulary constantly implies purposes where none exist, and the utilitarians used it without taking sufficient notice of this fact. A man does not cease to be the dupe of words because he writes clearly, if what he says is an error suggested by the ambiguities of ordinary language. Marriage, property, government and law are all institutions having social functions and satisfying human needs; nothing is easier than to talk of their 'purposes' and to imply that men established them for good and sufficient reasons. It is easy to see that if we were to lose them we should be much worse off than we are. What is less obvious is that many of the desires they satisfy were created by them, so that it is at least as true that we want them because we have them as that we have them because we want them.

These are considerations too obvious not to have occurred to such clever men as the utilitarians. Hume, when he destroyed the theory of the social contract, suggested that governments had arisen as a matter of convenience, with no one understanding quite what had happened, and that later they were accepted because every one felt they were indispensable. He supposed that, if government was created by convention, it must have been in the same way as language, which developed among men and was accepted by them because it occurred to nobody to do otherwise. Besides, the whole theory of association of ideas, as it was used by the utilitarians, implies that the individual is as much the creature as the creator of society. James Mill tried to show that all the social affections are produced by the association of ideas, whose operation so modifies the native character of men that it can scarcely be recognized under the second nature evolved from it. But though the utilitarians understood these things and made the most of them when it suited their purposes, they did not understand their full significance for political theory. The experience that determines the associations of ideas which make a man's character is itself a social product; neither its nature nor its causes are likely to be understood by that man, and yet because of them he is what he is. All that James Mill, or any other exponent of the theory of the association of ideas, can know is man as he is. Their opinions about how he came to be such are mere conjectures, having no scientific value. What, indeed, could be less scientific than to construct the notion of man, in abstraction from society, and then to explain society in terms of his desires? No doubt, since man is the only political animal, there must be something about him that explains this unique quality. But what this something is, is one of the last questions that political theory, sustained by a wealth of knowledge not yet at its disposal, can answer. To talk of instincts instead of purposes and desires is to come no nearer to the truth; it is merely to substitute empty words for error.

In discussing the 'individualism' of the utilitarians, I have been discussing only their method of explaining social phenomena. I have not been arguing that the state does not exist for the sake of individuals, nor yet that individuals exist for the sake of the state. These two statements are, in my opinion, equally misleading. To convert them into questions and to attempt answers is to lose time that could be wasted more agreeably. Does the state exist for the sake of individuals? It is clear that they never contrived it, and that without it they would not be what they are. They would not have the purposes they now have were it not that they are citizens. Do individuals exist for the sake of the state? This question, like the other, invites no answer. The state is not a person and can have no end, and it is unlikely that we exist for its sake. If these questions are worth asking, they must be addressed to God, who alone can answer them. It may be that He brought states into existence to make men happy and virtuous; or it may be that He liked the look of states and created men to make them possible. Here are two possibilities that the philosopher can contemplate, but he ought not to pretend he knows which is the more likely to be true.

I ought, perhaps, to add, so as to avoid misunderstanding, that the writers who have said, either that the state exists for the sake of individuals or the opposite, have often subscribed to one or two of four opinions, all of them plausible though not all compatible with each other. But none of these opinions (nor any combination of them) implies that individuals exist for the sake of the state or the state for their sake. These four opinions are: (a) nothing is intrinsically good except some experience or activity of an individual; (b) the state (i.e. the association of many individuals standing in determinate relations to one another) is intrinsically good; (a) there exist universally valid moral laws; (β) every moral code is the product of a given society, and it has no validity outside that society except to the extent that other societies are like it. Philosophers who have held opinion (b) have sometimes also believed that the state is a mind having purposes of its own, and that it can never be right for the individual to disobey the laws of his state. To make these conclusions appear more plausible, these philosophers have often asserted (β) as well as (b). But it is clear that neither (b) nor (β), nor both together, can imply, either that the state has purposes of its own, or that it can never be right for the individual to disobey the laws. On the other hand, what the utilitarians and many other

L

English philosophers have often asserted is also badly argued: that because the state is only an association of individuals, it cannot be good in itself but only as a means to the happiness, welfare or virtue of individuals. It may be that nothing is good except what is individual; but if this far from self-evident proposition should be true, it certainly is not proved to be so by the bare assertion that the state is not a person or a mind. Indeed, the proposition, though it may be true, is not as plausible as the other three. For we know that men's devotion to societies and institutions is usually out of all proportion to their belief in their utility. They love them for what they are and not only for the good they do to individuals. It is the crudest psychology to suppose that patriotism, or any other group loyalty, is the desire to promote the welfare of individuals. If we care for our fellow countrymen more than for other men, it is because they share our loyalties. We prefer our compatriots because we love our country; and we do not love our country for their sakes. Patriotism and philanthropy are as often at war as at peace, and they seldom collaborate. Civilized men like to reconcile the two, and they even pretend to derive the former from the latter. But in more primitive societies, it is the group and its institutions, the living together after a certain fashion, that men most value. And they value it for what it is, without so much as asking themselves how it affects the happiness, welfare or virtue of individuals. Those therefore who say that nothing is good but what is individual are committed to the opinion that what most people have always valued much more than the welfare of the immense majority of persons whom they know (not to talk of the ones that they don't know) has in fact no intrinsic value.

The first political thinker of modern times who, for at least as long as it took him to write one essay, left these two superfluous questions (does the state exist for the sake of individuals, or the opposite?) quite out of account was Rousseau. In his *Discourse on the Origins of Inequality among Men*, he gives an account of the birth and development of society, an account which he admits is conjectural but which implies a conception of the relation of man to society much closer to the truth than the one preferred by the utilitarians. According to this account, the use of reason and language go naturally together, and neither is possible outside society. From this it follows that, until man becomes a social animal, he literally does not know what he is doing. He is urged by his emotions and desires to actions of whose further consequences he knows nothing, and yet these consequences are the emergence and development of a society that profoundly modifies his character. It is true that a social contract is described in the *Discourse*, but it is also implied that the developments leading up to it and its own further consequences are alike outside the control of the men in whose actions they are manifest. Rousseau sets no store by the details of his account and is content to suppose that something of the kind may have happened. It was Marx who coined the phrase: 'It is not the consciousness of men that determines their being, but their social being that determines their consciousness.' The truth, thus clumsily expressed, was illustrated a century earlier by Rousseau, at considerable length and in less misleading language.

This essay, though perhaps the most original of Rousseau's political writings, is only a small part of them. In the *Social Contract* and elsewhere, Rousseau was untrue to the principle implied in the *Discourse*. It was Saint-Simon, who, among modern thinkers, first put its true value on the principle that human societies develop in accordance with laws unknown to their members, whose characters, beliefs and purposes are profoundly affected by that development. Saint-Simon, a careless and often obscure writer, never succeeded in stating the principle without at the same time suggesting much that is false. In one passage, he tells us that 'the supreme law of the progress of the human spirit dominates and carries everything along with it; men are only its instruments. Though this force issues from us, it is no more in our power to put ourselves out of the way of its influence or to control its operation than to alter the primitive impulse that makes our planet turn round the sun.'[1] Here is a passage that is as obscure as extravagant. What is this supreme law? If it is a law of the development of society, why call it a law of the human mind or spirit? The use of the word *progress* adds a touch of optimism that science can very well do without. And why should it be assumed, without qualification, that men have no power to control their future? To call men instruments is to suppose a purpose beyond them. It is not possible, by selecting quotations, to separate the dross from the gold in Saint-Simon's writings. The two are inextricably mixed together.

[1] *Organisateur*, IV, p. 119.

Like Marx, Saint-Simon was incapable of speaking without saying a great deal more than was true or even than he meant. And he had the added misfortune of writing in French, a language in which nonsense hardly ever sounds impressive. But the meaning of the passage I have quoted is, I think, clear enough. It implies at least this much: that societies develop according to laws that are not made by men; and that this development, though it accords with human nature, is not to be explained in terms of human desires, beliefs and purposes. It also implies a great deal more that is false. But many of these false implications are denied by Saint-Simon elsewhere, while the principle I have tried to enunciate pervades his whole theory and affects all his thought about political and social matters. 'The natural course of events' says Saint-Simon in another passage, 'brings to birth the institutions adapted to each phase in the development of society (nécessaires à chaque âge du corps social)'.[1] Or, in other words, these institutions are not human contrivances. From such premises as these, Saint-Simon argued to the conclusion that the method of the social sciences must be historical. Their purpose is to trace the development of social institutions and to determine their functions at any given stage of that development. It is not the purpose of these sciences to guess at the motives that lead individuals to obey governments and to accept conventions. Saint-Simon was never interested in the great problem that has exercised so many political theorists, both before his time and since; he was not interested in political obligation. He set an example from which we have not yet sufficiently profited. For surely, the beginning of wisdom for political theorists, if their study is ever to become scientific, is to understand that the problem of political obligation is not theoretically important. The true answer to it, though sometimes cleverly disguised, is always a platitude. It cannot be a case of the duty to keep promises, for the great majority never promised obedience. And if we say, with the utilitarians, that subjects ought not to disobey unless they believe that disobedience will prevent more evil than it occasions, we make a statement as useless as it is true. Or, rather, it is a statement that has only a negative utility; for if we believe it is true we shall not be tempted to say anything so astonishing as, for instance, that subjects must always obey their governments because the state is its own end.

[1] *Physiologie Sociale*, X, p. 190.

The utilitarians were right in thinking that, given that men have made up their minds what things are desirable, it is easy to lay down a general rule about the duty of obedience to and the right of revolt against government. At the level of abstract political theory, the problem of political obligation is simple enough. Which is not to say that it is not difficult in practice. Indeed it is, as all important problems are apt to be. To disobey or to seek to overthrow a government is to risk great dangers for uncertain benefits. Hume and Bentham did not deny the obvious; they merely saw that a rule which is difficult to follow may be easy to define. They saw that the fancy answers given in the past to the general question, Why should subjects obey their rulers? involved making un- necessary or obscure or unplausible assumptions: as, for example, that men have consented to government even though they do not know it, or that the state exists for the sake of the 'good life', or that there is an 'eternal law' written in all men's hearts limiting the authority of their rulers. Yet Bentham did not treat the question as deftly and simply as Hume did. True, he said that govern- ment exists to promote happiness, but he went on elaborately to define happiness as a sum of pleasures. He tied his theory of political obligation, not to a loose and popular and generally acceptable notion of happiness, but to a notion which seems the more fantastic the more closely we look at it. He contrives his account of the subject's duty to government in order to support a peculiar and unlikely doctrine about the supreme end of human endeavour.

If we compare the utilitarian theories with those of Saint-Simon, we immediately notice two things: the indifference of the utili- tarians to history and the little importance they attach to faith. In both these respects they belong to the eighteenth rather than to the nineteenth century. Hume was an historian, but he made only a small use of history to illustrate and support his political theories. Bentham and James Mill, like Voltaire, regarded history as no better than the record of the crimes and follies of mankind. They even took Voltaire's aphorism more seriously than its author had done. That history could teach the political theorist anything worth while was what never occurred to these two men, who condemned *a priori* reasonings and vulgar prejudices, and who always believed that their fundamental principles were generalizations from experience. Indeed, the political writings of even Hobbes and Locke (except when they are engaged in controversies of a semi-theological character), no less than those of the utilitarians, are remarkable for the small interest they exhibit in history and in the comparative study of societies. Even the extravagant and un-worldly Rousseau, at his most theoretical in the *Social Contract*, devoted a larger proportion of his few pages to comments on the contemporary world and antiquity.

When I say that the utilitarians attached little importance to faith, I do not refer only to their indifference to religion. I mean, rather, that they had no idea of how much men's behaviour is affected by their beliefs. Hume, it is true, said that all government rests on opinion, but he meant only that, if people did not think it their interest to do so, they would not obey their rulers. He never understood that, quite apart from religion, there exists in every society a whole system of prevalent beliefs and prejudices, peculiar to that society, without which it is impossible to explain the behaviour of its members. Men are selfish, generous, cowardly, brave, jealous, stupid and intelligent from one end of the earth to the other, and we learn nothing at all about the development of any society or its difference from another by contemplating the vices and virtues common to mankind. It is the beliefs and preju-dices that have no direct connexion with the general psychological characteristics of men (and that must be acquired, because they cannot be inherited, by any particular man), in which the political theorist is interested. It is they that are intimately connected with the institutions prevailing in a given society. It is, perhaps, the great merit of Saint-Simon that he understood this better than any man had done before him.

The individualism of the utilitarians, their explanation of social phenomena by a human psychology supposedly prior to society, also made them indifferent to social classes. They conceived of society as composed of a number of competing individuals and not of rival groups. They did not, of course, deny the existence or political importance of classes, nor did they fail to mention them when it would have been unnatural not to do so. But they found no place for them in their general theory of society. It seemed obvious to them that, as the result of competition, some must be rich and some poor; and since this must be so in the free economy of which alone they approved, they thought it no less desirable than inevitable. But the social and political consequences of this fact did not, except on occasion, interest them. They were out to destroy sinister interests, they objected to monopolies, and they, most of them, had no respect for aristocracy; but that the political and class structures of society are so closely bound up with one another that a change in the one can hardly occur without a change in the other, is an idea that meant almost nothing to them. They neither denied the fact nor understood its importance for the political theorist. That combination of ingenuity and indifference to fact, which is Hume's great defect as a moral and political philosopher, is nowhere more conspicuous than in his account of property. Bentham and James Mill, highly critical of aristocracy, hoped that democracy would make predominant the educated middle class to which they themselves belonged. They had their strong social preferences but no real understanding of the political importance of classes. They had read Plato and Aristotle but had failed to learn the most obvious lesson taught by them. It is again in Saint-Simon that we get the first modern account of how, as political systems succeed one another, the relations of the social classes to each other are altogether changed. He thought that, already in the twelfth century, with the enfranchisement of the communes and the emergence of the 'industrial' class, there began the great process that was to destroy the medieval world and to form, beneath the decayed remnants of the old, the strong and healthy structure of a new society. Only the last of the great utilitarians, John Stuart Mill, lived in a Europe already so much alive to Saint-Simon's ideas that it was impossible for an intelligent man to neglect them. It is the younger Mill of whom alone we can say that he was often willing to sacrifice logic to truth.

I have said enough about the defects of the utilitarians, defects from which the younger Mill, not only because he lived later, but also for temperamental reasons, suffered less than the others. They were common to the great majority of eighteenth- and early nineteenth-century political thinkers, most of whom lacked the great intellectual qualities of the utilitarians. As destroyers of nonsense, Bentham and James Mill had not the tact, elegance and economy of Hume. Yet they were shrewd and vigorous critics. It is to the English utilitarians, much more than to any continental

writers, that we owe our liberation from the political vocabulary
inherited from the middle ages. They did for political and moral
philosophy what the Cartesians did for the theory of knowledge.
They made some simple definitions that define nothing, and they
left a great deal too much out of account. But they also resolutely
set aside much that political theorists are the better for discarding,
and no serious student of the social sciences will think little of this
service. It is a great and indispensable, and always a difficult, service;
for men are most attached to nonsense in those studies that touch
closest to their lives. Where the undergrowth is thick and strong,
only the sharpest instruments and strongest arms can make the place
clean.

It was given to the utilitarians to clear the ground but not to lay
out the garden. And they have this grievance against their successors, that the garden is still barely visible and the ground almost as
encumbered as it was a hundred and fifty years ago. If it should
happen that they laboured in vain, the fault will be not theirs but
ours. A number of good ideas were born in the nineteenth century,
mostly in France. But who can say that in the social studies there
are now discernible the orderly progress and the large measure of
agreement which alone are evidence that a new science has come
into the world?

CHAPTER X

APOLOGIES AND CORRECTIONS

IT is a disturbing experience to have to read once again a book written by yourself many years ago and scarcely looked at since it was published. You read what you wrote as if someone else had written it, and yet not altogether so, for you also have the feelings of the man who hears his own recorded voice and is disconcerted. It is less disturbing to forget the past and to start anew than to have to pick it over and make amends for it. Though I have neither the time nor the inclination to write another book about the utilitarians, I have been given an opportunity to correct past mistakes—and also, no doubt, to make new ones. Having read my own book once again, I cannot refrain from taking that opportunity. It may be pleasanter to correct other people's mistakes than one's own, but the urge to correct one's own is stronger. As it clearly is not an urge to get pleasure or to avoid pain, merely to confess it is to throw doubt on the utilitarian philosophy.

The utilitarians and the other writers I have discussed were engaged in one or more of three kinds of intellectual activity: in explaining how we use certain moral and political (and also other) concepts, in explaining the origins and functions of social institutions, and in advocating certain forms of behaviour. Only the first activity is a part of philosophy in the narrower modern sense of the word; the second belongs to sociology and psychology; and the third may be called, for want of a better word, propaganda. It is true that propaganda, as we nowadays speak of it, is much more than simple suggestion or direct persuasion; it is also the advocacy of theories and opinions about matters of fact. It is propaganda because these theories and opinions are put forward as much to affect behaviour as to explain the world. Nearly all the utilitarians, though some much less than others, were propagandists; they gave practical advice and also elaborated theories which they hoped would induce people to take it. Of the four most famous utilitarians, Hume engaged more in the first and second of these three kinds of activity than in the third, Bentham more in the second and third than in the first, and the two Mills extensively in all three. In correcting what I have said about them and about other writers, I shall deal first with their philosophy, next with their psychological and sociological explanations, and last with only one part of their propaganda, James Mill's argument for representative government. I shall not confine myself to making corrections; I shall also add some new comments and criticisms.

1. PHILOSOPHY

I now think that I have sometimes been too absolute in choosing one rather than another among several plausible interpretations of a writer's meaning, or in emphasizing one part of a theory at the expense of others, or in contrasting one theory with another. This is, I think, particularly true of what I say about Hobbes and Hume.

I was interested in Hobbes as a precursor of the utilitarians, and therefore attended only to certain parts of his theory. I did not, as I should have done, confine myself to drawing attention to what is common to him and to the greater utilitarians; I also spoke as if what they had in common were somehow more authentically Hobbesian than what Hobbes shared with his contemporaries and with tradition, as if Hobbes the precursor of the utilitarians were the 'essential' Hobbes. I still believe that it would be possible to construct out of some of the elements of Hobbes's theory a coherent system without treating the laws of nature as either moral principles or divine commands and without postulating a contract. Hobbes could have supposed that the laws of nature were only maxims of prudence, and then, without either God or contract to help him, could have gone on to explain how completely self-regarding men might find it their interest to obey government. Yet the fact remains that he did not do so. The traditional aspects of his theory are as much part of it as the rest, and are not the less essential to it because it is possible to put together a more coherent theory without them. Moreover, the laws of nature of tradition, if they are contrasted too sharply with Hobbes's natural laws, are made to appear different from what they really were. For they were seldom thought of as purely moral laws; they often included prudential maxims and even descriptions of how men behave. The laws of nature of tradition were not even, all of them, rules of conduct, for men had not yet learnt to distinguish statements of fact from prescriptive sentences. Whatever seemed to them universal about man's behaviour, they were apt to call a law of nature, on the ground that man so behaved by 'necessity of his nature'. It can at least be said for Hobbes that his laws of nature, even if they are not moral principles, are properly rules of conduct. Though the law of nature of tradition has a large element of morality about it which Hobbes's natural law almost certainly lacks, it is also a less pure, a more mixed-up, conception.

I have spoken of Hobbes as if he were a hedonist, though some writers, among them Professor Oakeshott, have denied that he was one. I do not think that I was wrong, but I do think that I made too much of his hedonism. There are several passages in Hobbes which seem to imply that he was a hedonist, and none, so far as I know, which clearly imply the contrary. It is more likely that he was one than that he was not. Yet he did not make his position clear beyond possibility of doubt; and what is more, it does not greatly affect his general account of human nature and government, whether he was one or not. He spoke much more of security and danger than of pleasure and the avoidance of pain. He believed that man is by nature an egoist who always acts from hope of some benefit or fear of some hurt to himself. This is the belief that mattered most to him, and it need not be interpreted in a hedonist sense.

In my first chapter I say that the moral theories of Hume and James Mill are 'naturalistic' in Professor Moore's sense of the word. I should no longer want to say this—at least not of Hume's theory. A moral theory is naturalistic, according to Professor Moore, when it treats goodness as a 'natural' property; that is to say, either as a quality inhering in the things called good or as a relation in which they stand to something else. Professor Moore says that goodness is a simple, unanalysable, 'non-natural' property, neither constituent nor relational, but (as he puts it) 'resultant'. I do not think I have ever really understood what a 'resultant' property might be; for it seems to me that when we say that anything has a property, we are either referring to some quality inherent in it or else are saying that it stands in some kind of relation to something else. I am certainly not suggesting that Hume may have believed, with Professor Moore, that there are such things as 'non-natural' or 'resultant' properties. If Hume's moral theory is not naturalistic, it is still poles apart from Professor Moore's.

A moral philosopher is guilty of what Professor Moore calls the 'naturalistic fallacy' if he says or assumes that goodness is the same thing as one or other of the properties common to the things called good, these properties, inherent or relational, being all 'natural' in Professor Moore's sense. Now, it is possible for a philosopher not to do this and also not to treat goodness as Professor Moore has treated it, as a 'non-natural' property; it is possible for him to treat the word good as if it referred to no property of any kind. This, indeed, is what many recent writers on morals have done, and it may be that Hume did it. It is a possibility that I ought to have taken into account, though in fact I did not do so. Because it was obvious to me that Hume's philosophy has no place for what Professor Moore calls 'non-natural' qualities, I took it for granted that his moral theory must be 'naturalistic' in Professor Moore's sense. I now see that this need not be so.[1]

I do not want to go to the opposite extreme by suggesting that Hume's account of moral judgments can be assimilated to one or other of the accounts given by twentieth-century writers. I do not say that he believed that moral judgments merely give vent to feelings, or are commands disguised as descriptions, or are special forms of persuasion. These sometimes elaborate modern theories have been deliberately put together to meet difficulties not yet thought of in Hume's time. They make a bold front where Hume's position is uncertain, for they want to answer questions that Hume never put to himself.

Hume tells us, in many places, that we call a character or action good when the mere survey of it, without hope of profit or fear of damage to ourselves, gives us pleasure, and evil when the mere survey of it gives us pain; and this kind of pleasure and pain he calls approval and disapproval. He also says that when we call something good we 'express' approval of it and 'praise' it, and that when we call it evil we 'express' disapproval and 'condemn' it. Now, to say that we call something good when we feel about it in a certain way is not to imply that we use the word 'good' to refer to that feeling. Because, whenever anything gives me a certain kind of

[1] I had not read Mr. Stuart Hampshire's article on *Fallacies in Moral Philosophy* when I wrote this book.

pleasure, I call it good, it does not follow that, when I so call it, I am saying that it gives me that kind of pleasure. Hume never troubled to make it clear what he meant by saying that to call something good is to 'express' approval of it. When we say that we 'express' a feeling, we need not mean that we make a statement about it; we may mean only that we say something which gives vent to it and is a 'mark' of it, not in the sense of referring to it, but of being a conventional effect of it. Hume actually says that 'good' and 'evil' are *marks* of approval and disapproval, and says it in contexts suggesting that they are evidence that we have these feelings rather than references to them.

And yet there is at least one passage in Hume suggesting that the virtue of an action or character consists in its arousing a certain kind of pleasure. In the *Enquiry Concerning the Principles of Morals*, he says: 'The hypothesis which we embrace is plain. It maintains that morality is determined by sentiment. It defines virtue to be whatever mental action or quality gives to a spectator the pleasing sentiment of approbation; and vice the contrary.'[1] If we take the last sentence literally, it scarcely makes sense. Virtue can hardly be any action or quality which gives a certain kind of pleasure, for then it would be many different things. The natural interpretation of Hume's clumsy sentence is that the virtue of a 'mental action or quality' consists in its giving a certain kind of feeling to the spectator. And in the language of Hume's theory of morals, to call an action or quality virtuous is the same thing as to call it good.

It has been argued, for instance by Mr. Hare, that to approve of something is not to have a certain kind of feeling about it. 'If I ask "Do I approve of A?" my answer is a moral decision, not an observation of introspective fact.'[2] I doubt whether the answer to this question is always, or even often, properly a moral decision, but it is, I think, true that usually, when we put this question, we are not inquiring into the state of our feelings. But I suspect that Hume would have said that we always, or nearly always, were; for he had no doubt that approval is a feeling. His words often suggest that when we say that something is good we are not saying how we feel about it; but they never suggest that when we say we approve of something we are not referring to our feelings. It is

---

[1] Selby-Bigge. 2nd Edition. p. 289.
[2] R. M. Hare, *The Language of Morals*, pp. 6–7.

almost certain that he would not have agreed that moral judgments are imperatives put grammatically in the indicative form. Of course, he never asked himself whether they were so, but what he says about them does powerfully suggest that, if he had put the question, he would have answered that they were not.[1]

He would, however, have agreed—as all the utilitarians would have done—that the social function of moral judgments is to affect behaviour. Habits of approval and disapproval arise, he thinks, in order to encourage some kinds of behaviour and to discourage others. Men would never have come to make the moral judgments they do make if they had not been concerned about one another's and their own doings; and these judgments have a very powerful effect upon them. Opinions like these are not confined to the utilitarians; they are the common sense of mankind. Was there ever a writer on morals who would have rejected them? But it does not follow that moral judgments (distinct from overt moral rules) are imperatives merely because their social function is to affect behaviour, for we must always distinguish between the social and the logical functions of a form of speech, and also between both these functions and the actual intentions of any person who uses them. Thus we cannot conclude that Hume, who insisted so much that this is the social function of moral judgments, came close to treating them as if they were imperatives, without getting as far as saying that they were so. He believed that moral judgments are 'expressions' of feeling, and that we have learnt to use such 'expressions' because it matters to us that people should behave in some ways and not in others. If he had held consistently and unequivocally that moral judgments are statements about feelings, his theory of morals would be naturalistic in Professor Moore's sense. But he did not do so. More often than not, the actual words he used do not imply that when we make moral judgments we are speaking about our own or other people's feelings. That is why it is misleading to say—as I did say—that his theory is naturalistic.

It is less misleading to call the elder Mill's theory of morals 'naturalistic', for he nearly always makes the morality of an action (its goodness and its rightness, which he often runs together as if

---

[1] This may be a little misleading, for it is always possible that a man who has not put a question to himself would change his mind as a result of putting it. Indeed, this is one of the commonest ways in which we come to change our minds; we put a new question and then see that the answer in keeping with our present beliefs will not do.

they were the same) consist in its consequences. Sometimes, when he speaks of goodness distinct from rightness, he treats it as if it were the same as being approved of. In either case he commits Professor Moore's 'naturalistic fallacy'. He does not, however, always do so, for there are times when his position is much like Hume's. For instance, in his *Fragment on Mackintosh*, he says: 'Those acts the effects of which (men) observed to be beneficial (i.e. pleasurable or conducive to pleasure), they desired should be performed. To make them be performed, they . . . affixed to them marks of their applause; they called them good, moral, well-deserving; and behaved accordingly.' This clearly does not imply that, when we call an action good, we are referring to its consequences or to our feelings about it or to something inherent in it.

All in all, it was probably a mistake to bring Professor Moore's 'naturalistic fallacy' into a discussion of utilitarian moral theories. True, Professor Moore accuses the utilitarians, among others, of this fallacy. Sometimes, no doubt, they were guilty of it, for sometimes they did treat goodness as if it were a natural quality inhering in the things called good or some of their consequences or some kind of feeling towards them. But I doubt whether many of them did so at all consistently. All that I would now say with assurance is that none of them thought it a 'non-natural' quality in Professor Moore's sense, whatever that may be. Where, like Hume or the two Mills, they have a developed theory of knowledge, that theory leaves no room for 'non-natural' qualities; and where they do not, there is still no reason for believing that they thought of goodness as a quality of that kind. I fear that I allowed myself to be taken in by a tacit assumption on which several of the arguments in *Principia Ethica* rest: that a moral theory is 'naturalistic' in Professor Moore's sense if it does not give some such account of goodness as he gives.

In discussing John Stuart Mill's admission that some pleasures are better than others, I defend him against the criticism that by this admission he is false to his own doctrine that nothing is good but pleasure.[1] I say that if there were different kinds of pleasure, as there are different colours, then it would be possible to hold, both that nothing is good but pleasure and that some pleasures are better

---

[1] See Chapter VIII of this book, p. 137, and also Chapter IX, pp. 146–7.

than others, just as it could be said that nothing is beautiful except colour and that some colours are more beautiful than others. Though I admitted that there is no reason to believe that there are kinds of pleasure in the same sense as there are kinds of colour, I did, by using this argument in defence of Mill, suggest that he might have believed it. Actually there is no better reason for supposing that Mill believed this than for holding the belief oneself. It is true that Mill does say that 'neither pains nor pleasures are homogeneous, and pain is always heterogeneous with pleasure'.[1] The context, however, suggests that he is speaking of pleasant and painful experiences rather than of pleasure and pain; that he is saying (what is obvious) that there are many different kinds of experience, pleasant and painful, rather than (what is by no means so obvious) that there are different kinds of pleasantness and painfulness. The utilitarians ordinarily treat pleasure and pain as if they were simple qualities of the 'sensations' or 'feelings' called pleasant and painful; as if they stood to these sensations as redness does to red things. To defend John Stuart Mill as I did was to suggest that he might have believed what he almost certainly did not believe, and what is almost certainly false. If someone were to defend me in that way, I should not be pleased.

Most of the utilitarians did not trouble to consider what pain and pleasure are. Many of them lost nothing by this neglect, for they spoke of pleasure and pain as they are ordinarily spoken of, and there was no need for them to do otherwise to make their meaning clear. When they spoke of the pursuit of pleasure, they meant the pursuit of pleasant things; and though they called some pleasures greater than others, they did not suppose that it was possible to measure them. The utilitarians, Bentham foremost among them, who believed that we desire pleasant things on account of their pleasantness, and (more strangely) that pleasure and pain can be measured, would have done well to ask themselves just what pleasure and pain are. There are some quite simple questions which they must either have failed to put or else not have taken seriously; for if they had put them and taken them seriously, they could hardly have persisted in their beliefs. I have in mind such questions as: Are pleasure and pain themselves feelings which

---

[1] J. S. Mill, *Utilitarianism*, ch. 2, ¶ 8.

accompany other sensations, or are they properties of the sensations called pleasant and painful? If two pleasant or painful feelings differ in intensity, is the more intense always the more pleasant or the more painful? And if the answer to this question is *No*, can we still hold that pleasure and pain are qualities inherent in the feelings called pleasant and painful?

In Chapter XVII of his *Analysis of the Phenomena of the Human Mind*, James Mill considers pleasurable and painful sensations, and also sensations which are neither and which he calls 'indifferent'. He says: 'I have one sensation, and then another, and then another. The first is of such a kind, that I care not whether it is long or short; the second is of such a kind, that I would put an end to it instantly if I could; the third is of such a kind, that I like it prolonged.' How are we to interpret this passage? Does the pain of the second sensation consist in my wanting to put an end to it, and the pleasure of the third in my wanting to prolong it? This is what the context suggests. If that is so, it still has to be explained how pleasure can be an object of desire and pain of aversion. James Mill also says, not once but repeatedly, that to desire something is to find it pleasant and that to be averse from it is to find it painful. Thus, in at least one place he explains pleasure and pain in terms of desire and aversion, and in many others explains desire and aversion in terms of pleasure and pain. If he were asked to choose between these two positions, what would he say? It may matter to his analysis of the human mind that he should give one answer rather than the other; but to his utilitarian theory of morals, it matters very little. For either way, the conclusion as to what is involved in desiring pleasure must be odd and unconvincing. If to desire something is to find it pleasant, then to desire pleasure is to find pleasure pleasant; and if to find something pleasant is to desire that it should be prolonged, then to desire pleasure is to desire to prolong the desire that something should be prolonged.

I do not want to pursue these matters further, but only to suggest that Bentham and James Mill perhaps found it easy to be hedonists because they never seriously asked themselves just what it is we are saying about something when we call it pleasant or painful. They took it for granted that it is obvious. At the level of common sense it may be so, but not for the purposes of moral theory.

2. Psychological and Sociological Explanations

The utilitarians have often been criticized for their shallow theories about how the human mind works. If they had pushed their analyses further, if they had not been satisfied with their too simple views about what pleasure and pain are, or about what we really do when we praise and blame, they could hardly have persisted in holding that the pursuit of pleasure is the usual occupation of mankind, or that happiness can be defined merely in terms of pleasure, or that moral judgments are 'expressions' of feeling, or that they are statements about the usual consequences of actions.

The psychology of the utilitarians now seems to us woefully inadequate. Yet to insist on this, as I have done, can be unjust. No doubt, it is not possible to analyse all human experience, as James Mill tried to do, into 'sensations' (i.e., following Hume, into 'impressions' received through the senses and their faint copies or 'ideas'); to treat the mind as a kind of arena in which 'impressions' and 'ideas' combine in different ways. It cannot be shown how these combinations make up a human mind without tacitly assuming mental processes not to be explained in terms of them. Hartley, Helvetius, Condillac, and James Mill were all attempting the impossible: to explain the mind as a mere flow of sensations. It was not, however, enough to point this out, especially in a book which was as much historical as analytical. For these four men, inspired by Hume, were in their own day considerable innovators. Who before them had gone so far in analysing mental processes? Moreover, some of their explanations were subtle and ingenious. I have insisted too much on their inadequacy.

I have also said that the utilitarians were wrong in trying to explain social institutions as contrivances to satisfy human wants. I do not now want to depart from this judgment but only to qualify it. It has long been the habit of political and social theorists to speak of social institutions as if they were instruments devised by men; or as if they were solutions to practical problems, or means adapted to ends. Montesquieu and Burke have been praised for seeing that this is not so; that though society is no more than men living together and behaving in certain ways, and is merely a product of human actions, it is not what it is because men have decided that it shall be. It is an effect of innumerable human decisions and not a contrivance of human wisdom. Or rather, it is not, taken as a whole, such a contrivance. Yet at least Montesquieu, if not Burke also, would probably have admitted that men, having studied the society they live in, can reasonably endeavour to change it. Though what they can successfully do with it is always severely limited by what it is, it is not absurd or presumptuous in them, if they have studied it deeply, to seek to improve it. A community can change in either or both of two ways: when men, without bothering their heads about what it is like, in pursuing more limited ends, act in ways that change it; or when, inspired by some vision of what it ought to be like, they try to change it. Montesquieu and Burke both believed that change happens more in the first way than the second, and that the second is the more dangerous; though I suspect that Montesquieu was more willing than Burke to allow that it might be necessary.

Montesquieu and Burke, and also Rousseau, had a better notion than the utilitarians of what human communities are like. Yet the difference between them, great though it was, was not as great as my ninth chapter suggests. The utilitarians, though they often spoke as if social institutions were made by men for their own convenience, were aware that institutions change slowly, not only because it takes time for men to learn how to get what they want, but also because their wants change as a result of what they do to satisfy them. They knew that man is educated in society, and that this education moulds his character, providing him with habits, tastes, and principles he would otherwise not have. They knew also that every community is vastly intricate, that habits are stubborn, and that moral preferences, once acquired, are difficult to change. Though they too often spoke as if institutions were human contrivances, they were less taken in by this manner of speaking than I have supposed. If we compare them with the French revolutionaries and with Tom Paine, we find them much more cautious and more respectful of tradition; not only the conservative Hume but also the radical Bentham and James Mill.

In any case, it is no nearer the truth to speak of social institutions *growing* than to suggest that men have *made* them deliberately. They neither grow nor are made; they are the largely unforeseen consequences of deliberate actions. To say that they grow is to suggest that they have become what they are independently of men's

172 *The English Utilitarians*

actions; as if how they change were somehow determined by their original constitution, by what they were when they first appeared. The utilitarians never lost sight of the truth that institutions are only ways in which men behave, and that there is nothing about them which determines that they *must* change in one direction rather than another. It is not institutions that grow but men who give up some conventions and acquire others; and this is none the less true because men do not ordinarily decide upon their conventions to suit their needs.

There is no harm done in speaking of institutions either 'growing' or 'being contrived' provided we know what we are about when we do so. To avoid intolerable circumlocutions, we must, when we speak about man in society, use metaphors, and all we need do when we use them is take care that we are not deceived by them. When we contemplate society and consider how we may improve it, we fall easily into the habit of speaking of institutions as if they were instruments devised for our convenience. And so, to a limited extent, they are, especially in sophisticated societies. When, however, we compare our own society with others very different from it and see how much we owe what is peculiar to us to our social environment, it is easy and natural to speak of society as if it consisted of processes independent of our wills. Just as we do not decide what will happen to our bodies as they come to maturity, so we do not choose how 'society' shall influence our minds. In neither case do we control the processes in which we are involved, and so we come to speak of them in the same way, as if the second were also a kind of growth. In one sense, social processes are very largely independent of our wills, for we scarcely ever choose that they shall be what they are; but in another sense, they are dependent on our wills, for they are the ways in which we behave. When they change it is because people have either decided or been moved to behave differently. They are not what happens to us, as the growth of our bodies is; they are what we, as rational and wilful beings, do. In fairness to the utilitarians be it said that they were not more taken in by their metaphors than some modern sociologists are by theirs.

It is, however, possible to admit, as the utilitarians sometimes did (though less than they should have done), that men are as much creatures as creators of their social environment and still fall far short of the truth in describing what is involved in being a social creature. Though we allow that men's needs and ambitions differ greatly from society to society, and also that as society changes so too do the wants and interests of its members, we can still treat man as if he were no more than a subject of desires intent on satisfying as many of them as possible. This is how most of the utilitarians, with the important exception of John Stuart Mill, treated him. They admitted that man comes to have, in society, many wants that he would not have outside it. Most of them even welcomed this fact, for they believed that the greater men's wants are, the more they need one another's services and the more they value social peace. The utilitarians were not, with rare exceptions, champions of the simple life, and they mostly believed in progress. Yet in their eyes, however sophisticated man might be, however dependent on his fellows and well-disposed towards them, he always remains essentially a creature intent on getting as much as possible of what he wants, a kind of accumulator of satisfactions. They see him as an intelligent and provident subject of desires always in full pursuit of a happiness conceived as a train of pleasures. Society they look upon as a kind of market, a system of transactions whose function is to satisfy as many desires as possible at the least cost.

The inadequacy of this account lies, not only in its hedonism and the strong (though sometimes unconscious) bias towards egoism, but in the quite unreal conception of what a moral and social being is. Even if we suppose that men do not ordinarily desire pleasure and are often as much interested in other people as in themselves, the unreality of the conception remains. Man is not just an animal who, unlike the others, is provident and calculating; who can forgo satisfying present wants in order to put himself in the way of getting more of what he wants in the future; who, in the process of working with others for mutual benefit, comes to have more and more wants; and who acquires a set of moral standards to restrain him as a competitor and encourage him as a collaborator with others. He is a self-conscious, self-communing, animal who sees his life in the round, who knows that he must die, who is his own most constant companion, whose desires are often fantasies, who wants to be one kind of person rather than another and to live one kind of life rather than another. He is, as Hegel might put it, 'his own object'; he has some image of himself, more or less variable, more or less obscure, which it matters to him enormously should be true; some idea of what is proper to him or worthy of him. He is the happier and the more secure and easy in his mind, the more confident he is that the image is true and the better or the more impressive it appears to other people. Just as we are interested in ourselves as persons rather than as subjects of desire pursuing satisfactions, so too are we interested in others. It is as persons, much more than as competitors and collaborators for the satisfactions of wants, that we hate and love one another; that we feel pride, envy, and gratitude. Our wants flow largely from the ideas we have of ourselves and our neighbours, and of the kind of life we want to live. But the utilitarians, except for John Stuart Mill, speak as if the great object of our lives were to cater as best we know how for a multitude of desires; as if man were a collection or sequence of appetites, each to be fed in turn or to be sacrificed only to make the food go further.

We value freedom, so they tell us, because it is painful to us when our desires are thwarted. No doubt, it is painful. Yet we value freedom much less on account of this pain than because it matters to us that we should live one way rather than another; that we should be one kind of person rather than another. We are moral persons, not primarily because we follow rules which prevent our getting too much in each other's way as we strive to satisfy one desire after another, but much more because we try to see ourselves and our neighbours as whole persons leading whole lives. True, we do not see either ourselves or them as we and they really are; we are not in full possession of ourselves, or anywhere near it; we live fitfully and uncertainly and in a half-light. We do not exactly know what we want to be or how we want to live; our ideas are half-formed and change continually. Our heads float while our feet walk, and we are often closer to the real world in our habits than our thoughts. We are often vague and restless; but we are so precisely because we need much more to make us happy than to see our way to satisfying as many of our desires as possible. If we were really the sort of creatures that Bentham thought we were, we could be neither happy nor unhappy, but only more or less successful in the pursuit of pleasure and the avoidance of pain.

Because they thought of men as creatures pursuing one private end after another, the utilitarians made too little both of the quality of the inner life needed to make a man happy and of community of faith and shared loyalties. If all that really matters is that individuals should satisfy as many as possible of their desires in the order of their strength, then it matters how they live together, what kind of community they form, only to the extent that their living one way rather than another enables them to get more of what they want at the cost of less effort. It matters that John should get what he wants, and that James should get it, and William too; and John may care for James's welfare and William's as well as his own. Even if we allow for more than altruism, even if we abandon hedonism and allow that men care for other things besides getting pleasure and avoiding pain, we can still speak of society much as the utilitarians and the welfare economists do; we can speak of it as if it were a mass of individuals collaborating and competing for the more efficient satisfaction of a multitude of desires.

If, however, we suppose that men want more than to succeed as much as possible in satisfying one desire after another, their own or other people's; if we suppose that they also care what sort of persons they are, what figures they cut in the world, what kinds of life they lead, it is easy to see how they come to be attached to the community as much as to one another. How men see themselves, as they are or as they would like to be, is intimately connected with their mental images of the community; they are not mere competitors and collaborators, however benevolent, in a market for the supply of personal wants; they are members of society, and their hopes and feelings, both for themselves and others, would not be what they are apart from their group loyalties.[1] They see themselves as having rights and duties, as moral beings,[2] because they have some conception of a social world with parts for themselves and others to play in it. They would lack the affections and security which make happiness possible if they were not strongly attached to the community as well as to themselves and to other individuals. To Rousseau, and afterwards to Hegel,

[1] I do not want here to suggest that men are only social creatures, in the sense of creatures whose whole life is taken up by their relations with others; they are all often alone, and their relations with themselves may matter to them as much as their relations with others. These two kinds of relations are intimately connected; indeed, the 'interior conversation' whose quality mattered so much to Pascal is carried on to a large extent in the public language, in social symbols.

[2] I use 'moral' here to mean, not 'virtuous', but only 'claiming rights and admitting obligations'.

it seemed obvious that men could not be lovers of freedom, could not be deeply concerned that they and others should be able to live as seemed good to themselves, unless they were strongly attached to the community. This attachment, as they saw it, is more than a matter of feeling; it is a conscious sharing of beliefs which hold the community together, giving shape and substance to the lives of its members. It is as social creatures that men acquire the standards and preferences out of which they build up for themselves images, however vague, however inarticulate, however changing, of what they are and would like to be, of how they live and would like to live. These are the images that give them a sense of position and of purpose in the world.

Faith, in this particular sense, is not making assumptions or accepting conventions; it is a kind of communion with others of which only rational and self-conscious creatures are capable. From this it would follow that no one can totally reject the faith peculiar to his community, the standards that help make it what it is, and still feel loyalty to it. Loyalty to the community differs in kind from personal affection, and is not less necessary to happiness. This side of life, which meant so much to Rousseau and Hegel (and also to Burke), was taken almost no notice of by the utilitarians.[1] I now think this a more serious fault in them than their sometimes misleading habit of explaining social institutions as human contrivances for human ends. What they neglected is not a recent discovery; it was very much to the fore in the theories of several of their contemporaries. The utilitarians neglected it, not really because it was less obvious than what they did notice, but because they could not notice it and keep to their initial assumptions. When John Stuart Mill tried to take it into account, he never succeeded in squaring it with his utilitarian philosophy or in deciding just how much of that philosophy he should abandon to make room for it.

In my ninth chapter I try to make clear some of the defects of the utilitarian social theories by comparing them with the theories of Rousseau and Saint-Simon. If I had chosen Hegel in Saint-Simon's place, I might have done as well or better; but I was disposed, when I wrote that chapter, to think better of Saint-Simon than I now do

---

[1] I mean in their theories. What the theorist neglects is often as obvious as what he takes account of; and he often admits it, directly or by implication, when the requirements of his theory are out of mind.

and much worse of Hegel than was just or even excusable. Though the two have much in common, Hegel is the more systematic and the more profound, and even, I now think, the less obscure. For though he uses an extraordinarily difficult philosophical vocabulary of his own, he uses it consistently; it is possible to get the hang of it, to see how he uses it, and thus to discover what he is talking about when he happens to be talking about the real world. At least it is possible to translate his political and social theory into more ordinary language. Of course, the translation leaves out something which to Hegel would seem the heart of the matter; yet what remains is coherent, many-sided, and immensely suggestive. Saint-Simon was altogether looser and more confused, and as a psychologist, if not also as a social theorist, much more superficial. It is in Rousseau and Burke, in Montesquieu and Hegel, even more than in Saint-Simon, that we can find the best correctives of utilitarian psychology and social theory.

Speaking of Saint-Simon, I say that he was, among modern thinkers, the first to put 'its true value on the principle that human societies develop in accordance with laws unknown to their members'. I should now want to take out the words 'in accordance with laws' and substitute for them 'in ways'. Though Montesquieu and Burke were as well aware as Saint-Simon that men understand only a little the societies they belong to, they took no interest in actual processes of social change. Though Hegel described a number of phases in the evolution of the 'idea' of freedom, and also the actual societies in which (in his opinion) these phases are realized, he never troubled to explain how one type of society in fact changes into another. But this is precisely what Saint-Simon tried to do, albeit roughly, and he tried it on such a scale as to deserve to be called an innovator. He was a social historian in a way that none of the utilitarians were. He was erratic and slipshod, no doubt, but he did try to explain how European society had developed since the twelfth century of our era, and the attempt helped him to what was in many ways a more adequate conception of society than we can find among the utilitarians. I do not now want to go back on that opinion, but only to point out that the words I used are misleading. Saint-Simon spoke of a 'law' of social development; he spoke of human societies as if they were organic wholes with a pattern of growth proper to them. Whether this was exactly what

N

he meant, I now hesitate to say, for I feel even more strongly than before that he habitually used words carelessly without knowing what he was committing himself to by their use. But if he did mean it, there is nothing particularly valuable about it, and it is probably false. What is valuable is not the suggestion that human societies evolve according to some law but that they change in ways unknown to their members. To say that society changes is only another way of saying that conventional human behaviour does so; and there is no reason to suppose that change of that kind must happen in one way rather than another, or, in other words, that there is a set course or law of social development.

The writers who have emphasized what the utilitarians neglected have often put forward 'self-realization' as an end for man, and have made a difference between 'negative' and 'positive' freedom, calling the second 'higher' than the first. They have spoken as if there were for every man some condition of himself towards which he strives or ought to strive, and which he could or would attain were it not that ignorance and adversity prevented him; they have spoken of man's being most completely or essentially himself when he attains it, and have said that freedom is not so much absence of constraint as the opportunity to reach this condition. They have usually taken it for granted that the condition is broadly similar for all men, though also to some extent peculiar to each man, because men are broadly alike in their capacities and yet also different. These ways of speaking, though perhaps first invented by philosophers, are by no means confined to them; they have become common currency in the West, at least among the educated. They serve to express important feelings and aspirations, and are part of the practical vocabulary of morals and politics. It would be out of place to object to them in ordinary discourse on the ground that they are vague, for they are now almost indispensable metaphors. We know what they mean in the sense that we recognize the feelings and aspirations they are used to express. If we dismiss them as nonsense, we risk doing what many of the utilitarians did; we risk neglecting a large and vital part of human experience.

At the same time, if we try to use them to explain that experience, we risk talking nonsense; for we are then apt to take them literally, forgetting that they are at bottom only metaphors. We cannot

argue from the qualities that distinguish man from the other animals
to any condition of himself in which he is most 'completely' or
'adequately' human. Nor can we say, as Rousseau did, that there
is a kind of society or a kind of life that suits man better than any
other, in the sense that it alone enables him to be happy and to live
at peace and friendship with his neighbours. What a man can
become is, of course, limited by both heredity and environment;
but this does not mean that there are not, in any one type of society,
several different conditions of himself which could bring him
happiness, self-respect, and the good opinion of other men; several
kinds of life, interior and social, which he would find worth living.
And if we take more than one type of society into account, we can
extend indefinitely the number of conditions of himself or kinds of
life in which a man might be 'self-realized' in this sense. If, then,
we say that he strives or ought to strive to realize himself, we point
to nothing definite. There are, no doubt, certain capacities (for
instance, speech, abstraction and inference, deliberate choice, moral
and aesthetic judgment, etc.) which nearly all men acquire in any
society, and which we can hardly imagine them having if they had
lived in solitude; but these capacities are acquired as much by people
who fail to 'realize' themselves as by people who succeed. We
cannot infer from these capacities common to men in all societies
what society should be like or what kinds of behaviour should be
enforced or encouraged to enable men to 'realize' themselves.
Before we can give content to the notion of 'self-realization' or
'self-fulfilment' or 'developing capacities to the full', we have first
to decide what to aim at. I 'realize' or 'fulfil' myself, presumably,
not when I become what I am capable of being (for whatever I
become, I do at least that), but when I become what I most want
to be, provided that I do not regret having become it, which I
almost certainly will do if it makes me contemptible to myself or
to others. What I want to become and what makes me contemptible or respectable depend, in large part, on the rules of conduct
and standards of excellence of the communities I belong to. These
rules and standards are partly imposed on me, especially in childhood, when I am made to behave myself in ways convenient to
others; partly acquired by unconscious imitation; and partly chosen.
However I come by them, I cannot have a conception of a life
worth living without them. They can make either for happiness

or unhappiness. I may be satisfied with myself and my lot in one environment, and when I pass into another I may become dissatisfied. I may have a rigid character, and stick to the ideals and standards I have made my own in spite of a change of environment; or I may be softer and insensibly acquire new ideals and standards. In either case I may become unhappy: in the first because I reject my neighbours' standards and suffer their hostility, and in the second because I am not able to live up to my new standards. Or I may acquire incompatible standards and socially induced needs without being able to set myself to rights by giving up some of them.

The moral theories of the utilitarians are defective, not because they make no use of the notion of 'self-realization' (which is perhaps more dangerous than useful as an explanatory device), but because they take no account of the experience which that notion is used to explain. Those who use the notion have therefore one great advantage over the utilitarians, that they do not neglect an important part of man's behaviour as a social and moral being; but they have also a great disadvantage, that they raise spurious problems. Where the utilitarians fall short of the truth, they go far beyond it.

They also go beyond it when they distinguish between two kinds of freedom, positive and negative, bringing into their account of the first kind their beliefs about what makes men put a value on freedom. There is much to be said for these beliefs, but there is nothing gained by suggesting that men are deprived of freedom only when their 'higher' impulses are thwarted. True, every man has a legion of desires, many of which he never attempts to satisfy, so certain is he that, if he did, he would be prevented. Every man distinguishes among his own desires between the permissible and the forbidden; and also between those which he keeps hidden merely to avoid censure and those he is ashamed of. Not only does he try to satisfy his shameful desires, even when they are stronger, much less often than the others, but he also resents it much less when his attempts to satisfy them are thwarted. We are often, perhaps usually, more angry at being prevented from doing what we do not think it wrong to do, even though our desire is mild, than at being prevented from doing what we are ashamed of, even when our desire is strong. As soon as a man has some image of himself as he would like to be or some conception of a life worth living, he has strong preferences among his desires, approving of some because they accord with this image or conception and condemning others because they do not. Often, when the desires he condemns are thwarted, far from complaining that he is deprived of freedom, he is relieved or even grateful. No man's desires enjoy parity of esteem, even in his own eyes.

If we want to explain why this is so, we cannot do it as Bentham and James Mill tried to do. It just is not true that we sacrifice some desires to others, or esteem them less, merely because they are weaker, or because to satisfy them would lead to painful consequences, or because we fear that by satisfying them we shall put it out of our power to get what we are likely to want in the future, or for some other such reason. Our preferences among our desires are not determined only by their strength, their frequency, their probable effects, painful and pleasant, and so on; but are governed rather by what we want to be and how we want to live, or by what we want other people to think of us. We should not have these strong preferences among our desires if we were not rational and moral creatures; and it is because we have them that we resent some impediments to action much more strongly than others, even when our motives are much weaker. The impediments which we most resent and wish to remove we single out for condemnation as restraints on freedom, expecting and demanding of others that they should not put them in our way.

All this is true. Yet it does not justify our defining freedom as absence of restraint to our 'higher' impulses. Our scale of values, though always deeply affected by current moral codes and standards of excellence, may not accord with them exactly or even nearly. Again, these codes and standards are not always compatible with one another; so that what a man takes from them can sometimes bring him into conflict with some or all of his neighbours. He may be perverse or wicked, and yet be none the less a social, rational, and 'moral' creature on that account; though 'moral', of course, only in the sense that he has his own preferences, passing value judgments according to standards acceptable to himself. He has ambitions and ideals, and not just desires some of which are stronger or more frequent than others. Though it is what stands in the way of his ambitions that he condemns as restraints on freedom; though he makes claims on others, not so much because he wants as few obstacles as possible in the way of all and sundry of his desires as because he wants to reach and hold on to some ideal of a life worth living; though it is as a 'moral being', as a maker of judgments of value, that he acquires this idea; though all this is so, it is still misleading to call the desires connected with this ideal 'higher impulses'. They may be nasty or dangerous. Nor can we plausibly say that the man is not restrained in his freedom unless these desires are higher impulses; for that is to speak against the common sense of mankind.

We should conclude, I think, that the idealists were right as against the utilitarians in holding that it is primarily as a moral being, and not merely as a provident subject of desires (who, because he cannot satisfy them all, satisfies some rather than others in the hope of eventually satisfying as many as possible according to their strength), that man comes to demand freedom, but that they were wrong to define freedom as absence of impediments to the higher impulses. We ordinarily mean by freedom either our not being prevented from doing what we please or the right not to be prevented. It is one thing to explain how we come to claim and cherish this right, resenting some restraints much more than others, and quite another to explain how we use the word freedom. The utilitarians attempted both explanations. Though with the first they were further from the truth than the idealists, with the second they were nearer.

Even if we agree with the utilitarians that the first moral rules were only rules of convenience, that men came to prescribe some forms of behaviour and to prohibit others because they discovered that by so doing they could get more of what they wanted more easily, we can still reject both their hedonism and what, for want of a better word, I venture to call their 'actuarial' or 'statistical' conception of morality; that is to say, their belief that the social function of all moral rules is to enable men to satisfy, at the least cost in effort, as many as possible of their desires. For we may hold that 'convenient', in this context, means, not 'making for pleasure' (including in pleasure the avoidance of pain), but 'conducive to people's getting what they want', and that there is no good reason for believing that men, if they were not social and moral, would only want pleasure or other things for the sake of pleasure. We can

also argue, as I have tried to do,[1] that men, in the process of becoming social and moral beings who prescribe rules of conduct and
make judgments of value, cease to be mere provident creatures of
appetite bent on getting (whether for themselves alone or for others
as well) as many satisfactions as they can, and become persons who
see themselves living in a social world, framed and encompassed by
it, comfortable or uneasy in it, and who, as travellers through a
whole course of life, need to look respectable or impressive in their
own eyes and other people's. They do not, of course, make to
themselves a single, clear, and comprehensive image of what they
would like to be and do, and spend their lives trying to live up to
it. The image is always vague and changing; or rather there are,
at any period of life, several images, more or less vague, more or
less compatible with one another, and which all change with the
years. If there were, at any stage in life, one fixed image, or several
that never changed or were incompatible with one another, men
could not suit their ambitions to their outward circumstances or to
alterations, physical and mental, in themselves. Yet, to be happy,
a man must have some such image or group of images and be able
to live up to it or them; he must be able to play the part or parts
he has cast for himself. Happiness, as the common sense of mankind has it, is 'contentment with one's lot'; and the 'lot' here in
question is not a Bentham's sum of pleasures but a course of life,
which a man may see as several strands or as a well-knit whole, and
be equally content either way, provided the strands in fact lie
snugly together or the whole is what he takes it to be. And to be
unhappy a man must have, not an excess of pain over pleasure, but
the sense that he is not what he would like to be, living as he would
like to live; or the sense that he does not know, though he feels
he ought to, how he should live and what he should be. He may
have strong appetites with the means to satisfy them, and yet be
unhappy. Any living creature can have pleasure or pain, but only
a moral being can be happy or unhappy. This we can say without
joining the ranks of the moralists who have held that the moral law
is discovered by intuition or by inference from the 'essential' nature
of man; we can even say it and still agree with Hume and James
Mill that moral rules arose in the first place from the 'necessities' of

---

[1] Following Rousseau and the idealists, but trying to avoid whatever in their
theories seems to suggest entities and purposes whose existence is doubtful.

mankind, and were solutions to practical problems rooted in our natural appetites. That only a rational and moral being can be happy or unhappy has been a common opinion ever since men began to reflect on morality and happiness. Indeed, even the utilitarians ordinarily took it for granted; and it was only in their moral theories that they either implicitly denied it or took no account of it even where it was clearly relevant. Theories, especially moral and social theories, often ignore what is generally admitted, even by their makers!

3. The Utilitarian Argument for Representative Government

I shall consider James Mill's argument for parliamentary or representative democracy only in outline. I now doubt—as I did not when I wrote the sixth chapter of this book—whether a convincing case for democracy can be made on utilitarian assumptions alone, even if they are not questioned.

It is true that the utilitarians nearly all believed in equality. But they did so in a sense peculiar to themselves. They did not discriminate among human desires except in terms of their consequences. No matter what a man wants, he should get it, provided his getting it does not prevent more pleasure than it occasions; for what he wants either is pleasant or he wants it as a means to what is pleasant. No human being is intrinsically superior to another and no sort of life is in itself better worth living. Therefore nobody has a right to rule others on the ground that he is a better kind of person or knows better than they do what is worthy of human nature. If he is skilful at producing happiness and wants to produce it, he has a claim to rule on those grounds alone. If we accept utilitarian assumptions, the burden of proof is always on whoever would prevent anyone getting what he wants. The function of morality is to enable as many people as possible to get what they want as often as possible. Moral rules are like traffic rules in at least one respect: they exist to help all desires, no matter what and no matter whose, to reach their destinations. If any are deflected or kept off the roads, it is only to keep traffic in general flowing more freely. Some utilitarians, among them Bentham and James Mill, put it forward as the fundamental moral rule that the traffic of desires should be as heavy and fast as circumstances allow: for that is really what their greatest happiness principle amounts to, if we assume, as they did, that men always desire pleasure or the avoidance of pain. Though there is no greatest happiness principle in Hume's philosophy, there is the explicit belief that the primary (if not the sole) function of moral rules is to enable people to get what they want as successfully as possible, and sometimes also the assumption that what they want is either pleasure or other things for the sake of pleasure.

To accept the greatest happiness principle is, of course, to reject many of the traditional arguments for aristocracy and monarchy: the arguments assuming that some kinds of persons and some ways of life are in themselves better than others. Yet the principle does not entail democracy, though some people have spoken as if Bentham and James Mill, arguing for parliamentary reform, were merely taking their utilitarian philosophy to a logical conclusion. If Hume remained always a conservative, his doing so certainly had nothing to do with his not putting forward the great happiness principle; for that principle favours no particular system of government. Hume believed that despite men's predominant selfishness, government is apt to be least careful of the public good when it is democratic. For the essential function of government is to protect property. It is the interest of all that the rules of property should be respected, for they arose in the first place because they were found generally useful. Unavoidably, these rules have enabled some people to get much richer than others, so that the rich are now often objects of envy to the poor. It is therefore better that the rich should rule than that the poor should do so. Not because the rich are wiser or more virtuous than the poor, but because their immediate interest accords better with the public interest. If property is not respected, eventually all classes will lose more than they gain, but immediately the rich will lose a great deal and the poor may gain something. Hume seems to have taken it for granted that rules of property which were generally useful when they first arose continue to be so whatever inequalities they lead to.

Bentham and James Mill lived at a time when it was less easy to believe that the interests of the governing class squared with the public interest. There was an obvious conflict of interest between the landowners who had political power and the manufacturers who had not. There was also a conflict of interest between reformers with a reputation to make by serving the public and various privileged corporations. Rulers, said Bentham and Mill, will always prefer their own good to the public good, whenever they have to choose between them, unless it is contrived that they cannot pursue the first without also pursuing the second. The way to do this is to make them responsible to the people generally by extending the parliamentary franchise. Bentham and Mill did, however, admit that this device will not always have the desired effect. If the people are so ignorant as not to know their own interest, then governments responsible to them will have no motive for pursuing that interest, they will either do what the people want or what they can be persuaded to put up with. Representative government is therefore the best of all forms of government as soon as the people generally know their interest. Man's preference for himself over others is rooted in his nature and therefore incurable, whereas ignorance can be cured. If rulers are not responsible to the ruled, nothing can be done to ensure that they prefer the public interest to their own, when the two diverge; but the ignorant can be taught their own interest. Thus the recipe for good government is this: Educate the people and give them the vote.

It is this argument that I now want to consider rather more closely than I have done in my sixth chapter. Representative government is ideally the best because, whereas 'selfishness'[1] is incurable, people who are ignorant of their interest can be taught to know it; that is to say, they can by education be put in the way of discovering it for themselves.

I find this argument unconvincing for two reasons. It makes a false inference from the premise that 'selfishness' is incurable; and it ignores the immense difficulties in the way of anyone's discovering his 'interest', if 'interest' is defined as it must be to make sense of the great happiness principle. Or even to make sense of a simpler rule which could be substituted for it: Do what will ensure that people get what they want as often as possible. Bentham and James Mill would have taken this second rule to be equivalent to

---

[1] I use the word 'selfishness' because it is simpler to do so, though at some risk of confusing the reader. James Mill held that everyone always prefers his own good to other people's, but he also distinguished between selfishness and unselfishness. His business, as a moral philosopher, was not to deny a distinction universally made but to explain it. By 'selfishness' I mean, in this context, not what is ordinarily meant, but what the utilitarians sometimes called the 'self-preference principle'.

the greatest happiness principle; and though it clearly is not (unless they were right in believing that what men want is always pleasure and the avoidance of pain), we can assume that it is for the purposes of our argument.[1]

In the philosophy of James Mill 'selfishness' is incurable by definition. It is 'human nature' to prefer your own good to other people's, and to say that anything is 'human nature' is only another way of saying that it cannot be changed. The people are just as 'incurably selfish' as their rulers. It is not 'selfishness' but its evil effects that can be cured. Why, then, should we hold that it is easier to cure the evil effects of government's 'selfishness' by educating the people than by educating their rulers? The public-spirited ruler is as much selfish, in this broad sense, as the self-indulgent tyrant. He is public-spirited because he behaves according to standards that promote the public good. Is there any reason for believing that the best way of ensuring that he does so is to make him responsible, directly or indirectly, to the people? No doubt, if he is responsible to no one, he is likely to abuse his power. That is the opposite extreme. Between responsibility to all and to none, there are, however, innumerable possibilities. A select ruling class, specially trained like Plato's guardians, are responsible only to one another for how they behave. This kind of responsibility may ensure good government more effectively than representative democracy could do, and perhaps also more cheaply. It certainly does not follow from the 'incurable selfishness' of mankind that the Platonic method is the less effective. Granted that the guardians of a Benthamite community would need a kind of training very different from what Plato described in the *Republic*, it might still be easier to provide this training for a small part of the community than to make most people good judges of their own interest. Once it is admitted (as it is by James Mill) that men can be trained to be public-spirited without ceasing to be entirely 'selfish', there can be no argument from human 'selfishness' to representative government. It is then merely a question of comparative costs. Is it easier to train your rulers to be public-spirited or to make good citizens

---

[1] It will, I hope, become plain to the reader, in the course of the argument, that, if it holds with the substitute rule, it must hold with the greatest happiness principle; and the substitute rule is the simpler.

of the people generally? James Mill's account of human nature helps not a whit towards answering this question.

His argument looks better than it is because we are so often disposed to speak of a group or class as if it were an individual. If a man is never responsible to anyone for what he does, he is apt to behave badly. But to say of a group of persons that they are irresponsible is only to say that they are not responsible to outsiders. They may well be (and usually are) responsible to one another. Whether their behaviour is or is not in keeping with the public good depends on what they expect of one another, on the standards they maintain. Furthermore, the ruling class can scarcely ever be treated as a single group; for they usually consist of many groups whose members are often highly critical of each other. The kind of responsibility that makes government public-spirited may depend less on democracy than on freedom of discussion among the small part of the people who do not govern but take an intelligent interest in public affairs; and this freedom is not necessarily the greater, the more democratic the form of government.

What could be meant, in utilitarian terms, by a man's 'knowing his interest'? It clearly could not mean his knowing what he wants, for that he always does. The utilitarian psychology leaves no room for the subconscious. According to James Mill, to have a desire is to know that you have it. To know his own interest a man must know what will make him happy, and his happiness depends on his continued success in getting what he wants, satisfying as many as possible of his desires and leaving as few as possible unsatisfied. To know his interest, a man must know, in a general way, what he is likely to want in the future; he must have an idea of the relative frequency, importance to himself, and so on, of his future desires. His knowing what he now wants takes him almost no way towards this other knowledge; for to have it, he must understand what sort of person he is and is likely to become. Also, he must know what is likely to happen to him, for his wants will change with his circumstances. At the best, if he has self-knowledge and sensible opinions about his future, he can know roughly what he will want for a few years ahead. But this is still not enough; for he must also know what has to be done, by himself and others, to ensure that he gets what he is likely to want. If he knows that, he knows his own peculiar interest about as well as he can hope to know it.

Yet even this does not suffice for his happiness. Other people have their interests, and he cannot expect always to get his own way. To know all that he need know to secure his interest, he must know what has to be done to adjust his interest with other people's; or at least he must know whom to choose to do the adjusting for him. If everyone were to judge government with only his own interest in mind, there could be nothing gained by making government responsible to the people; for a man must take some notice of other people's interests before he can decide wisely who is to adjust his interest with theirs. Now, it is hardly possible for anyone to know his own interest, if interest is thus defined; and yet it must be thus defined to square with the utilitarian philosophy.

If we want to talk sensibly of interests and their adjustment, we must treat a man's interest, not as the condition of his satisfying his desires as often as possible, but as whatever serves to maintain or improve his position in society. His interest can be adjusted to other people's, not because his success in satisfying his desires can be measured against their success, but because, when his demands conflict with theirs, it is possible to reach a settlement. To say that interests have been reconciled is only another way of saying that the settlement reached seems just to all the parties to it.

For a man to know his own interest,[1] he need not have self-knowledge or much understanding of his social circumstances; all he need know is what people situated as he is think they are entitled to, and whom to turn to for advice and assistance. He need not know what government should do to maintain or improve his position, or to reconcile the claims of people like himself with the claims made by others. True, his position in society may be unique, and no one else may make exactly the claims that he does. He may be the only postman in his town who is a Catholic, a married man with six children, an ardent philatelist, and a member of the Labour Party. No other man will make quite the same demands on society as he does, but the demands that he makes will all depend, more or less, on what demands are commonly made by people situated, in one respect or another, as he is. He will know the more easily whom to turn to for advice and assistance, whom to vote for as a spokesman for one or other of his several interests, precisely because

[1] By a man's interest I mean, in this context, the claims he can reasonably expect government or persons having some influence on government to take notice of.

he shares each of these interests with other people. There are accepted standards for estimating the competence of advocates and negotiators. If, however, 'interest' is taken in the utilitarian sense, there are no such standards. How can I decide who can best help me to satisfy as many as possible of my desires? Many people have devoted time and thought to such a question as: What must be done to improve the lot of miners? But who, except John Smith, cares about John Smith's getting what he wants as often as possible? Does even John Smith care?

People come to clamour for democracy when they come to want things that they did not want before; and democracy, when it comes, encourages them to ask for still more. It also makes it more likely that real efforts will be made to satisfy these demands. What the poor and unlettered ask for, when they come to be discontented with their lot, is usually what the rich already have. Democracy does therefore tend to 'level up'. It creates new wants and provides the means of satisfying them. But we cannot say that it increases happiness (in Bentham's sense of happiness) unless it satisfies more wants than it creates.

Until the voteless begin to ask for the vote, there is little reason to believe that they would be the happier for getting it. And when they do ask for it and get it, there is little reason to believe that they are happier (or more successful in satisfying their desires) than they were before they began to ask for it. While they did not ask for the vote, they probably did not want the things that the vote may bring them. Not until the voteless come to want what their rulers wish to prevent their having, have they anything to gain by getting the vote. They begin asking for the vote[1] because they come to believe that it is the means to their getting something else they want, or because they are persuaded that it is their due, or for both these reasons. There are social conditions of various kinds that favour their acquiring these beliefs; and we can therefore say that, when these conditions hold, there is a good chance that people will be made happier, at least for a time, by being given the vote. But there is no reason for believing that, when these conditions hold, people 'know their interests' any better than when they do not

[1] Often, of course, they get it without asking for it, especially in 'backward' countries that have 'progress' thrust upon them. Even when not asked for it is often welcome, if the voter, who gets it for nothing, is paid for using it.

hold. This is equally so, whether we take 'interest' in the Benthamite sense or in the quite different sense, which I have tried to define and which I believe to be closer to ordinary usage.

One country is not better governed than another when happiness is more increased or when government is more successful in enabling people to get whatever they want. If this were the criterion of good government, we could seldom in practice have sufficient grounds for holding that one country is better governed than another. A country is well governed when the claims that people make on government or on one another can be settled in ways that are generally accepted as just and proper. There is thus no need for a country to be democratic in order to be well governed. We can say only that it needs to be democratic in order to be well governed, when the people make claims that governments would not meet unless their power depended on popular vote.

If we suppose that all that matters is that interests should be satisfied as efficiently as possible, we may be driven to most unwelcome conclusions. This may be so, whether we take interests in the sense I have defined or in the sense of Bentham and James Mill. If all that matters is that interests should be satisfied, why should not government take it upon itself to decide what interests people shall have? Why should it not induce people to want what it suits their rulers that they should have? These questions are as much in place when we are thinking of people's social ambitions, their concern to maintain or improve their position in society, as when we are thinking, unrealistically and in the manner of Bentham and Mill, of the whole gamut of their desires. For if government can provide people with ambitions or desires more easily satisfied than the ones they already have, it is surely a duty to provide them. Once again, it is a question of comparative costs. Is it easier to get people to want what you can give them, or to try to give them what they want? Which of the two is easier depends on circumstances. It may be that, with the resources available to government in Bentham's time and Mill's, it was easier to do the second than the first; but it may now be that the first is easier. If that is so, then surely government ought to do it?

To avoid such unwelcome conclusions, we must qualify our definition of good government. We must say that a country is well governed when the claims that people make can be settled in ways that are generally accepted as just and proper, provided that government does not take it upon itself to decide what people's moral standards shall be. This, of course, does not mean that government must not see to it that people are properly educated by existing standards. It is not easy—and luckily it is not my present business—to decide what limits should be set to government's control of education; and I use the word 'education' in the broadest sense to cover whatever is deliberately done to ensure that people have some opinions, preferences, habits, and so on, rather than others. But some such limits there must be, if we are to avoid these unwelcome conclusions.

Why do we find these conclusions unwelcome? Not because we believe in happiness. It may be true that, in the modern world, governments, unless they are responsible to the people, will abuse their power by conditioning or 'brain-washing' their subjects. The abuse does not consist in their making their subjects less happy, for the more successful the conditioning the happier their subjects are likely to be; it consists in their treating their subjects as we think men have no right to treat one another. Therefore, before we can argue plausibly for democracy, we must assert a moral principle that the utilitarian philosophy takes no account of; a principle having nothing to do with the successful adjustment of interests— unless, of course, a man's interest is so defined as to include his freedom. We must do what Locke did; we must assert an ultimate right to freedom, though we need not call it 'natural' or define it as Locke did. We can, of course, assert this right without being committed to democracy; but we cannot make a really strong argument for democracy in the modern world unless we assert it.

I do not, for a moment, suggest that this principle or right meant nothing to James Mill and Bentham. They were moral creatures of the West European and English variety long before they were utilitarians. I find it easy to believe that there was more to their practical morality than they put into their theory of morals, and even that their theory was affected by that morality in ways unknown to them. If they had been, say, Chinese utilitarians, they might perhaps never have been moved to contrive a utilitarian argument for democracy. But that is another matter. I have been concerned only with the logic of that argument.